Our Best Life
before
the Best Life

Our Best Life *before* the Best Life

A Guide to Dating, Sex, and Marriage

Barnabas Kwok *and* Allie Kwok

RESOURCE *Publications* · Eugene, Oregon

OUR BEST LIFE BEFORE THE BEST LIFE
A Guide to Dating, Sex, and Marriage

Copyright © 2022 Barnabas and Allie Kwok. All rights reserved. Except for brief quotations in critical publications or reviews, no part of this book may be reproduced in any manner without prior written permission from the publisher. Write: Permissions, Wipf and Stock Publishers, 199 W. 8th Ave., Suite 3, Eugene, OR 97401.

Resource Publications
An Imprint of Wipf and Stock Publishers
199 W. 8th Ave., Suite 3
Eugene, OR 97401

www.wipfandstock.com

PAPERBACK ISBN: 978-1-6667-3518-5
HARDCOVER ISBN: 978-1-6667-9200-3
EBOOK ISBN: 978-1-6667-9201-0

MARCH 17, 2022 11:39 AM

"Scripture quotations are from the ESV® Bible (The Holy Bible, English Standard Version®), Copyright © 2001 by Crossway, a publishing ministry of Good News Publishers. Used by permission. All rights reserved."

Contents

Preface | vii

Introduction: Who We Are | ix

Chapter 1
The Waiting | 1

Chapter 2
Dating Worksheet | 5

Chapter 3
The Sign | 13

Chapter 4
What is Love? | 23

Chapter 5
First Encounter—Kona | 29

Chapter 6
Second Encounter—Hong Kong | 42

Chapter 7
Engagement | 51

Chapter 8
What is Sex for? | 58

Chapter 9
Third Encounter | 66

Chapter 10
The Best Life | 77

Chapter 11
Our Best Life | 84

Preface

Our Best Life before the Best Life captures the extraordinary story of a young, married couple: Barnabas and Allie Kwok. Their story serves as a testimony of God's power and sovereignty in orchestrating their quest for biblical love and godly marriage. Everyone who has heard of how they met and how the Lord moved in their relationship have been awestruck. They have shared their story in Christian circles as well as with an international magazine.

This book is structured as an interchange between testimony (narrative) and teaching. Most chapters are narrative, capturing their personal stories in both of their perspectives (Introduction, 1, 3, 5-7, 9, 11). The remaining chapters (2, 4, 8, 10) will touch upon the Christian worldview regarding dating, love, sex, and marriage.

In terms of teaching, this book touches upon the fundamentals of a healthy and prosperous relationship. As most people on this planet are on a quest for love and happiness, this book presents philosophical and practical means for a long-lasting and loving relationship in God's presence.

Introduction
Who We Are

BARNABAS & ALLIE:

We were dating by our first encounter, engaged in our second, and married in our third—stretched out across nine months of long-distance relationship. At the height of our dating relationship, we had an 18-hour time difference. Allie began work when Barnabas was about to go to bed, and Barnabas got off work when Allie was sound asleep. On our wedding day, we experienced many "firsts": the first kiss, the first time we saw our fathers cry, and the first time we shared a bed (in the sense of chapter 7).

But before we get into this extraordinary story of how Jesus joined us together through crazy signs and wonders, we would like to let you know about who we are—and how different we are from each other!

BARNABAS:

I'm a wanderer. Perhaps we are all wanderers since our home is with God in heaven. But really, I have never stayed in one home for more than 3 years straight. Born into a godly Christian family, I experienced my first change when I was 3 years old because my parents, Simon and Pearl (though they went by different names in different countries), were called to missions. We left Hong Kong

INTRODUCTION

(where I was born) and went to Singapore, then Mongolia, and continued to travel across Asia for the next 7 years as my parents proclaimed the Gospel of God. Being a missionary kid and third-culture kid, I ended up going to 15 schools in my entire life until this very point. I've been in public, private, Christian, Catholic, secular schools, and was even homeschooled—schools with thousands of people to a school of one; that is, me. I have been to tropical countries without winter, and countries where winter and snow dominated most of the year.

Yet, in the midst of all the constant change and inconsistencies, such as always being the new kid in a new environment, God has been with me. In fact, I came to realize the loneliness that was a result of my upbringing actually grounded me in putting my faith and dependence in Christ alone.

The most consistent thing that I was familiar with was God's faithfulness and power. I witnessed my grandfather—on his deathbed in the hospital—saying that he would not become a Christian unless he did not die that day because of cancer, only for God to heal him and live for years afterward as a born-again, Bible-believing, Christ-centered follower of Christ. He was filled with peace as he passed with a smile. I witnessed my mother get into a terrible car accident where she landed head-first onto the ground and immediately fell into a coma, only to rise a week later and refute the doctors' prediction that she would either die or live in a coma until death. I witnessed the Lord tell me through multiple people that He would pay 100% for my college tuition as a Bible and theology student at Biola University when it was financially impossible for my family to do so—only for Him to fulfill this 3 months before the commencement of my freshman year.

Even at my lowest point where I was friendless, bullied in middle-school, and chained to sin, I found myself in an empty locker room because my idol, soccer (or, as most countries call it "football"), couldn't save me. In the midst of that darkness and utter emptiness, the Lord met me there and radically transformed my life. From that point onwards, I became a born-again believer.

Introduction

My life is Christ's, and His life is mine; just as the apostle John records Jesus saying:

> "I have said these things to you, that in me you may have peace. In the world you will have tribulation. But take heart; I have overcome the world." (John 16:33)

I have come to find myself a wanderer, but not as a hopeless and restless orphan, but one with joy, hope, and peace that comes through the Spirit of God who lives in me and reminds me that my Christ—my King—has overcome the world.

Allie:

I have also been a wanderer but not in the physical sense of moving from place-to-place. In fact, until marriage, I had lived in the same house my entire life in a small town called "Kona"—famous for our beautiful beaches and flavorful home-grown coffee. Life is slower on an island: the speed limits, the building developments, the way we walk and talk, and even the food service. Do not be surprised if you order a meal and it takes much longer than expected, after all, you are on Hawaii time.

Growing up, my day-to-day life was routine, and I always knew what to expect. My biggest transition as an adolescent was when I decided to change schools from my sheltered charter school to public school. The reason? I felt out of place. My mom would pack me sushi for lunch but when I brought it out, my classmates pinched their nose, saying: "Ew! What is that? It smells and looks gross." Embarrassed, I dumped my food in the trash. When we had our eye exams, a classmate smirked as made his way towards me, "Hey Allie, I think you need glasses. I mean, how could you see out of those things?" Mockingly, he stretched his eyes with his fingers making it appear slanted and walked away.

I believed transferring to a new school would give me a chance to revamp my image and finally find a place where I belong. And for the most part, I really was able to change my image. Instead of the sweet, obedient, and timid girl I once was, I became mean-spirited, rebellious, and bossy. I painted over my eyes with thick black eyeliner, almost like a racoon. Every week I dyed my hair a new color: red, blue, purple, green— you name it. Classmates bullied me for my style, so I hissed back at them like a wounded animal. I became overdefensive, constantly putting up walls to not get hurt. The reality was that, even after changing my image externally, I still felt internally lost and out of place.

High school hit, and I made a 180-degree turn. Instead of my edgy middle school "alternative/emo look" I opted out for a "kawaii" style, which means "cute" in Japanese. Every day, I wore long dolly fake eyelashes, baby pink cheeks, and cherry-red lip tint. I refused to be caught wearing jeans, but only short fluffy dresses with frills and ribbons. For the next four years of high school, I devoted my time to studying Japanese with the hope of moving to Japan after graduation, finally being in a place where I belong. I was not bullied by classmates anymore and some even adored my style; yet, I still felt disconnected from them.

It was the second quarter of senior year and my parents wanted to speak about my future, "Allie, I don't think it's financially possible for us to send you to Japan for college." An uncontrollable rage boiled within me, and my body shook with anger. *Why have I wasted four years of my life studying Japanese then? What am I even doing? Where will I go? If only I could just live in Japan, my life would be different.*

My whole world changed. Suddenly, all those years of wandering and trying to find my identity came tumbling down. "Who really am I?" I fell flat on the floor of my room, sobbing. I did not grow up in church, nor have I even tried to read the Bible. But in my brokenness and despair I cried out in hiccups, "I feel so alone. I need You, Jesus." It was as if I was drowning, but suddenly, Jesus lifted me up from the depths of the ocean. I was saved. My tears ceased, and I ran to my mom's room, yelling: "I can't believe it, Jesus is real!"

That was over four years ago that Jesus saved me, changed my life, and gave me a new home: a place where I truly belong–His abiding presence for eternity.

Chapter 1

The Waiting

ALLIE:

No one ever told me that it gets lonely as a Christian. After Jesus radically changed my life at 18 years old, I lost quite a few friendships. Perhaps it was my overwhelming zealousness for the Gospel, begging friends to come to church with me. Or maybe it was the way that I began to talk, walk, and look—a life truly transformed by God. People began to distance themselves from me and say, "I miss the old Allie. She was a lot more fun. I hope this is just another one of her phases." My heart burst and I cried over their souls: *"Don't you realize? I love you even more than before because of Jesus' love, I so desperately want you to experience the love and joy of Christ."*

Summer came to an end and I began my journey at a Christian university. If anyone has been to a Christian school, you might have heard the term "ring by spring" or "gottem before autumn." But for me, it was the second to the last thing on my mind. As time passed by, there were people who began to express their interest in me. One of them asked to meet me privately. I uneasily agreed and immediately regretted it after he asked me out. I politely declined, but he persisted more, "I feel like God is telling me that there is a future with us. I'm going to keep waiting for you until you like me." I blinked, and then I blinked twice. *What? I did not hear about this from God.* The Bible instructs us to test all spirits (cf. 1 John 4:1), and I knew that was most likely not from the Holy Spirit. I apologized and awkwardly exited the scene by running off into the night alone.

On the other hand, there was a time where I was interested in someone and I prayed about it. That same night, I had a terrible dream about that person. When I woke up, all my romantic feelings for him were gone. The Lord told me "no" in pursuing any romantic relationship with him. There were also times when I initially met someone, I would already know whether or not this person would be suitable for me as a potential spouse based on their character and faith (chapter 2 will discuss this more). I knew that the next person I dated would be the one who I wanted to marry. After all, what's the point of dating if you're just going to break up eventually?

While I was able to make valuable and God-honoring friendships at this Christian university, at times, I still felt waves of loneliness. It was two in the morning and I couldn't seem to fall asleep. Maybe it was the caffeine from the latte I drank earlier pumping in my blood, or perhaps it was the overwhelming amount of stress I was feeling about school. Regardless of whatever it was, I put on my sweater and left my dorm to be greeted by the crisp evening air and smoggy Los Angeles sky. As I walked, I hummed praises until I arrived at my favorite place on campus: the prayer chapel. I poured out my heart to God and surrendered all fear, worry, and stress. I felt comforted knowing that He sees me and knows me in such an intimate way that no one else will ever know. I feasted upon His Word, holding on to it as my very hope.

This was just a glimpse of the many nights I had during this season of loneliness. Looking back, I thanked God for that season as I have had some of the most intimate moments with Him. Each cry-out to God, whispered prayer, soft hum and praise, built up my faith on a foundation depending on Christ alone.

BARNABAS:

Ever since I became a born-again believer in 8th grade, I made a vow to the Lord that I wouldn't date anyone until college. I suppose I thought dating relationships in high-school generally don't last until marriage, and that I should first focus on Him and "grow in the grace and knowledge" of Christ my Lord (cf. 2 Pet 3:5; 3:18).

By God's grace, I was true to my vow and I didn't date anyone throughout high school even though opportunities arose. There had certainly been times where I was only a thread away from dating, but God would miraculously intervene. Somehow, everything just wouldn't work out. One iconic instance was near the end of senior year when I got rejected by someone whom I thought wouldn't reject me. As I found out on a double-decker bus in Hong Kong after school, I remembered feeling terrible and amazing at the same time. Why? Because I was praying that it wouldn't work out, as I knew my interest in her wasn't for marriage even though my heart was constantly craving for a relationship—for a "love" that wouldn't satisfy. (Chapter 4 contains more on "love")

Then came college, which meant that I could finally date someone. Guess what, I was also at a Christian university... which meant most of my sisters in Christ were potential candidates, right? That ended up not being the case, and I came to realize that finding a suitable spouse was not easy. If a hardcore American republican would find it difficult to date and marry a hardcore American democrat because of massive conflicts regarding their worldviews and values, imagine how much harder it was for me as a missionary and third-cultured kid. I am a melting pot of various cultures and values, let alone some complexities with my theology and experiences in the faith. I realized this through a memorable conversation I had in the cafeteria during my freshman year. After sharing my testimony and all the amazing works that God has done, instead of praising God, this sister in Christ denied and challenged all my experiences as she believed that God did not do such things anymore. When I said, "God healed me," she replied with, "You don't really know that." Well, I did, and she didn't.

To help myself know what I was looking for in a future spouse, I made a Christian dating worksheet, which really helped me narrow down the type of person that I believed God was calling me to marry. There is a modified version of this worksheet at the end of this chapter—and I believe it can benefit you too.

Still, I was in a waiting season for three and a half years. I would cry out to God almost every day about this issue, especially when I believed that God had prepared someone perfect for me—not that she's perfect, but that God had truly chosen us to be joined together for His will to be completed through us as one flesh. I can't remember how many times I felt utter hopelessness and despair because I didn't have a girlfriend, even when other aspects of my life were full of God's blessedness.

One recurring theme that I experienced during the waiting was satisfaction. As hinted above, I wasn't satisfied, and I don't remember how many times my parents—who serve as my life-long mentors and godly example—had to remind me to find satisfaction in Christ, that He was my all in all. Could I boldly claim that God gave me Allie when I had mastered finding satisfaction in Him as a single man that was always on the move? No. But I can confidently assert that my quest of finding satisfaction in God—going all-in for Him and trying to involve the Spirit in everything that I did—as a single man was one of the most transformative times of my life. The amount of sin that vanished and the spiritual closeness with God that I experienced in college, particularly my sophomore and junior years, was amazing. I felt a powerful and tangible presence of God being all around me as I tried to place Him as my sole desire.

Chapter 2

Dating Worksheet

Here's the worksheet; more explanations will follow:

Category	(1) Relationship with God	(2) Personality and Character	(3) Background-Related Factors	(4) Confidence and Peace in the Spirit (or "God's approval")
Description	2 points: if most requirements are met (4 or more) 1 point: if half of the requirements are met 0 points: if most requirements are not met (less than 2)			4 or 0
Points	/2	/2	/2	/4
Total points:				/10

Purpose and Basis:

Perhaps contrary to what culture says about dating, that a person can only know whether or not one's partner is suitable or compatible *after* they are together—perhaps even living together—we believe otherwise. As a married couple, we are constantly discovering new things about each other. However, our core values, worldviews, and faith in Christ (what we believe about who Jesus is) has always remained the same. With the premise that dating is ultimately for marriage, we believe that one can know a lot about what another believes and values without committing to a dating relationship. This can be derived from the way one acts on social media, in social gatherings, at church, and even during dates (which is different from "dating").

We also believe that God deeply cares about whom one dates and marries, and that one's quest for love isn't based on luck—but God's will. While this is not imperative in every biblical account of marriage, there are at least four stories where we can clearly see God's will being involved when it comes to the finding of a spouse:

First, in the marriage of Isaac and Rebekah (Gen 24), Isaac's servant asked God for a specific sign for him to know whom the Lord has chosen to be Isaac's spouse (24:11-15). Genesis 24:14 writes:

> "Let the young woman to whom I shall say, 'Please let down your jar that I may drink,' and who shall say, 'Drink, and I will water your camels'—*let her be <u>the one</u> whom you have appointed for your servant Isaac*. By this I shall know that you have shown steadfast love to my master."

What happened in the story was that, before Isaac's servant had finished praying (24:15), everything that he had prayed for happened right in front of his eyes (24:16-20). God had answered Isaac's servant's requested sign perfectly, and not even Rebekah's parents could say anything because "the thing has come from the LORD; we cannot speak to you bad or good" (24:50). Rebekah shortly became Isaac's wife (24:67).

Second, in the marriage of Boaz and Ruth, we see divine appointment through unlikely "coincidences." When Ruth loyally followed her mother-in-law to Bethlehem to obtain leftovers for food (2:1-3), she "coincidentally" happened to arrive at Boaz's field (2:3), catching his attention (2:5-6). Boaz then happened to be one of Ruth's next of kin, enabling him to marry her (3:2; 3:12; 4:8-10). God divinely orchestrated all these "coincidences" so that Boaz and Ruth would marry. This became significant as they would eventually be in the line of David and Christ (Matt 1:5).

We won't go into detail concerning the other examples, but in short, God appointed His prophet Hosea to take a wife (Hos 1:2), and commanded Joseph to marry Mary through an angel (Matt 1:18–24). Both instances clearly evoke God's will in the Hosea's and Joseph's marriage.

These stories don't necessarily imply that your story of marrying your godly spouse will be in the same way as these biblical characters. But if God has done it before, He can do it again, and there are tons of stories capturing how He has clearly revealed His will regarding who He joins faithful believers together. Oftentimes, crazy stories of how the Lord joins two faithful believers together involve purposeful and prayerful waiting and selection. They did not just casually date around for the sake of dating; rather, they waited in accordance with God's standard of finding a good and godly partner.

Therefore, this worksheet is here to help you think through and assess whether the person that you are interested in, or the person whom you will be interested in, is suitable for you. If you are already married, this worksheet does not apply to you, but we believe this could be a good resource to pass on as a reference for those who could be going through a season of dating.

INSTRUCTIONS:

This worksheet is split into four categories with a total of *10 points*. The four categories are: (1) Relationship with God, (2) Personality and Character, (3) Background-Related Factors, and (4) Confidence in the Spirit (God's approval). In order for the person you are interested in to be "qualified" for you to date, that person is advised to have at least *8 points*, with at least one point in the first category.

Each of the first three categories has 6 requirements. If the person meets most of the requirements, then he/she receives 2 points. If half of the requirements are met, the person receives 1 point. If the person fails to reach most of the requirements, then 0. As for category 4, the person can only receive 4 or 0.

CATEGORY 1: RELATIONSHIP WITH GOD

1. *Personal Relationship with God:*

    Does this person have a relationship with God? Is Jesus the center of his/her life? Does this person experience intimacy with God through prayer, Scripture, and worship?

2. *Testimony:*

    Does this person have a testimony that involves a clear-cut transition indicating when he/she became a born-again believer? Does his/her testimony touch upon sanctification—how the Lord has gradually changed one's life in holiness and honor?

3. *Christology:*

    Who is Jesus Christ and who is He to this person? Can this person explain who He is with Scriptural support?

4. *Soteriology:*

    Does this person know how and why he/she is saved? Does this person know what he/she is saved from and what he/she is saved for?

5. *Pneumatology:*

    What is the relationship this person has with the Holy Spirit? How does this person view the Holy Spirit? Are you both in alignment with your views regarding the Spirit's work today?

6. *Ecclesiology (communal relationship with God):*

    What does this person believe about church—the people of God and the body of Christ? Does he/she belong to a local body?

Category 2: Personality and Character

1. *Fruit of the Spirit:*
   Does this person display the fruit of the Spirit as enlisted in Galatians 5:22–23? Does this person understand what love is? (see Chapter 4)

2. *Humility:*
   Does this person display a humility and meekness that reflects his/her acknowledgement of the person's spiritual "lack" and "need" for God?

3. *Responsibility and Diligence:*
   Is this person responsible and diligent in taking care of his/her life? Is he/she a hard worker?

4. *Sober-Mindedness and Observance:*
   Does this person have a strong sense of what's biblically right and wrong? Is he/she able to watch and discern what the Lord takes pleasure in and what He doesn't?

5. *Modesty:*
   Is this person modest in the sense that he/she is not focused on promoting and displaying himself/herself? There's nothing wrong with making yourself known, but the question is: Does this person display modesty in the sense that he/she desires to magnify Christ in everything he/she does? We would like to propose this question: what kind of person do you think you'll attract if you are focused on only presenting the external aspect of yourself: your body, face, and clothing? Would you be able to attract someone who will love you for who you are—your soul—your internal qualities and character?

Category 3: Background Related Factors

1. *Attraction:*

    Do you find this person physically attractive and appealing? Do you know why you are physically attracted to this person?

2. *Career:*

    Are your future career aspirations compatible? How compatible are they and may they not match up? If one desires to do global business and requires constant traveling overseas, but the other desires to serve the small church one was raised in, perhaps that's a conflict that needs to be worked out.

3. *Culture:*

    Are there any cultural differences and habitual practices that hinder your relationship? Is there a language barrier?

4. *Class:*

    Can both of you accept and be compatible with each other's social class (if there are differences)?

5. *Family*:

    What do your parent's think of the feasibility of this relationship? Can you get along well with his/her family (parents and siblings) and vice versa? Do your ideals for a family align with each other?

6. *Peers*:

    Do you have your peers' (perhaps even your brothers and sisters at church) approval to commence this relationship? How do they regard the person you're interested in?

7. *History*:

    What type of past does this person have, especially when it comes to dating? Is there anything that I can accept or not accept regarding this person's past?

Category 4: Confidence and Peace in the Spirit (or "God's approval")

This category is a little different from the previous three, because it's "all or nothing" for this one. You can either get 4 or 0. This means that, even if the person scores a 6/6 for all the previous categories, if you don't feel the Spirit leading you to date this person or if you don't feel a peace that comes from Him, maybe it means that he/she isn't quite suitable for you. Since we believe that God has a clear will for whom you are to date and not date, having a God-given confidence is highly important.

But how do we know God's will? This is where it gets complicated, but here are a few thoughts. First, this is *not* the same as the passion one experiences for another when one is in love. Again, while the biblical examples are not necessarily paradigmatic, the likes of Isaac, Ruth, Hosea, and Joseph did not experience God's will because they were so in love with the other person. In fact, in those cases, it was often the exact opposite. God isn't an emotion nor is His will only revealed through internal emotions. Oftentimes, God makes clear His will through external means.

This leads to the second point, that is, are there signs or experiences that could be interpreted as divinely orchestrated or a "God-thing"? Consider the biblical examples above and the rest of our story as an example. Third, in your current friendship and understanding of this person, do you have confidence and peace in your friendship as well as in the prospect of both of you being together in a committed relationship? Think about the supernatural peace Joseph experienced when the angel affirmed Mary to him as his wife.

Fourth, consider 2 Corinthians 11:2,

> "For I feel a divine jealousy for you, since I betrothed you to one husband, to present you as a pure virgin to Christ."

Contextually, while this passage refers to the relationship between Christ and the church, the imagery presented is that of marriage. Hence, one way to discern whether your relationship will have God's approval is to envision whether or not, as you present your boyfriend/girlfriend to others, you can present him/her as someone whom you are proud to be with–as a pure virgin to Christ, without blemish!

Concluding Remarks:

At the end of the day, this worksheet is just a tool to help you seriously ponder about any potential relationships. This worksheet isn't perfect, nor does it cover everything that one would should consider in finding a potential partner, but hopefully it can help you think about what a biblical relationship should be like.

However, we would like to remind you that this worksheet goes both ways; and perhaps, before you use it to evaluate others, it should serve as a mirror for you to evaluate how "date-able" or "marriage-material" you are.

Chapter 3

The Sign

BARNABAS & ALLIE:

It was the summer of 2018, Barnabas saw a friend's Facebook post on theology and felt prompted to comment. After multiple rounds of exchange, this post caught Allie's attention and she was captivated by Barnabas's view. Perhaps out of character, she decided to send him a friend request. Barnabas gladly became her friend on Facebook, and we soon began talking about God and Scripture. As we kept dialoguing on Facebook messenger almost every day for around 2 months, we were slowly developing feelings for each other.

ALLIE:

Ever since I returned to Hawaii for the summer, I received a lot of messages from different brothers in Christ. One night, while lying in bed and gazing at my phone screen, I began to feel uneasy. *What kind of testimony would I have as a Christian woman if I'm known to talk to so many guys?* Feeling convicted, I erased all my social media applications so I could focus on my relationship with God and build up my testimony. While I enjoyed my conversations with Barnabas, as they were very fruitful, deleting all of the apps on my phone also meant we would no longer be able to remain in touch. The only thing that remained on my phone was a Bible app.

While it wasn't easy cutting off social media completely from my life, I wrote two letters in my journal to Jesus on September 9th, 2018.

> A letter to my First Love:
> Dear Lord,
> I love You. You're all I need. Without You I have nothing and I am nothing. I want to know You. I want to know everything about You. How can I become close to You? How can I know You? Everything on earth will perish, but You are eternal. You will never leave me, Lord. My First Love, You are even right by me. There is nothing to fear. You are my provider. Thank you, Lord Jesus.
> Love,
> Allie

> A letter to my second love:
> My Lord,
> You are my provider, protector, deliverer, and Father. If You are willing, please allow me to get married to someone You want on Your timing. Now that I leave this matter into Your hands, I will wait on You. Please, I do not want this idol of marriage. I love You.
> Love,
> Allie

After cutting everyone off, I felt a bit bad for Barnabas as he seemed like a genuinely good guy. Being the internet detective that I am, I was able to find his email address and sent a brief explanation about my decision to obey God in devoting myself to Him. At the end of the email, I even mentioned that I wouldn't respond to him.

BARNABAS:

As Allie suddenly disappeared from social media, I gradually fell back into a state of gloom, heightened by how I had to leave my parents in Hong Kong and head back to the States for my junior year of college. It was truly a blessing to study God's Word at Biola. But at the same time, it still felt at times as if I was in a foreign land with various limitations, such as not being able to drive. Furthermore, as we texted through Facebook messenger almost every day for the past month or so, I thought "something was going on" and that maybe she was the one whom God had prepared for me all along. The email she sent me right before cutting me off gave me a glimmer of hope . . . but I felt like it was the same old experience I've had for the past 3 years in college—that I was back to my loneliness even though God has been faithful and close by my side.

We disconnected for almost two months, and on a Sunday during the middle of October, I just couldn't do it anymore. Honestly, nothing particularly unpleasant happened and I believe I had a good time at church, serving in worship. Yet, once I got back to my dormitory, I jumped onto my bed and cried to the Lord: *"I can't do this anymore, Jesus. Where's the person that you told me to wait for?"*

In the midst of such pain, emptiness, and despair, the Lord spoke to me. I generally consider myself as one who has a pretty-good relationship with God, as I would receive words and impressions from Him regularly. For instance, one time when I had to teach a class as my professor's teaching assistant, I felt the Lord told me not to drink coffee, contrary to my daily routine. I hesitantly obeyed. When the time arrived, I was filled with a strong presence of the Lord that was far better than coffee that spurred me to do well.

Still, what happened that Sunday was nothing like that. I had heard an audible voice from God that told me to "go find Allie."

I probably froze for a few minutes on my bed as I heard the Lord speak. *Wait . . . is this really from God?* I re-examined myself. Before the Lord spoke, I had almost given up on Allie as a potential spouse; but this experience changed everything. There was also nothing to lose as the worst outcome was that I would receive no reply. Thus, I immediately rushed to the library and penned an email to her.

ALLIE:

Two months into my fast from social media, people began wondering what I was up to. One of my friends said that it was like I disappeared from the face of the earth. The truth was I wasn't far from disappearing from the face of the earth as I worked at a place I never imagined myself to be: a fast food restaurant. Among all the jobs I've been at, from working at a clinic to even banking, nothing quite beats this one in terms of stress. I was constantly in a state of panic with the crazy amount of orders that came through. Not only were we greatly understaffed, but I would often work until midnight finding myself physically and emotionally exhausted.

I worked as the drive-thru operator, but ended up taking on other responsibilities such as receiving front orders, prepping and bagging food, and vigorously sweeping the floor all while speaking with a customer through our old intercom. "What was that? You wanted a cheeseburger without the cheese? Would you like a hamburger instead?" I asked. The customer frowned through the intercom, "No! I said I want a cheeseburger with no cheese, no tomato, and no mayo. I don't want a hamburger." Truly, this experience taught me to bite my tongue.

Life was once again boring and unchanging. Out of the blue, I received another email from Barnabas. I was shocked! It has been around two months since I last heard from him. I was surprised he was still willing to send a second email as I did not respond to him previously. Since a lot has happened since we last talked, I figured it wouldn't hurt to at least reply this time.

BARNABAS:

From that point onward, we started exchanging emails every day. And mind you, these weren't 300-word emails that briefly asked about our day, but 3000-word emails that covered everything in the dating worksheet in chapter 2 and more. We talked about our personal walks with God, our personalities, and backgrounds. Writing each email took me around 2 hours.

In one particular email, we talked about our Myers Briggs personality types. I am an ENTJ while Allie's is an ENFP. I immediately looked up how compatible we were and realized that, at least on paper (or, from the internet source that I was browsing on), we were a perfect match. At that exact moment, I told the Lord: "Lord, I don't know what's happening . . . but I don't know if I'll ever meet someone so perfect as her in my life." *Maybe we're meant for each other? Maybe she's the one whom the Lord has prepared for me?*

ALLIE:

By mid-November, we were still faithfully communicating daily through email. Sometimes I would respond to him through voice-memos and videos. Barnabas usually replied via email and occasionally voice memos. However, on November 21, 2018, Barnabas finally replied with a video. I sat on the carpet, back leaned on the dresser, and laptop seated on my knees as I played the video. He wore a grey sweater and a black scarf around his neck, "Hello! As you can see, I'm responding to your video with a video..." As I continued to watch the video, God spoke to me and said, "That's your husband" four times.

I was in complete shock and even denial. *No! That can't be my husband. I don't even know him. NOO!* I fell on my knees in prayer, "Lord if it is truly Your will for us to get married, may I be able to respect and honor Barnabas." I was flustered and scared, but held onto the words that God had spoken to me. I decided it would be wise to not tell a soul until I saw it come to fulfillment.

BARNABAS:

We kept on talking and everything was going well. We had even sent each other gifts and unofficial love letters. I was definitely in love with her. Since Allie told me that her plan was to continue her sophomore year at Biola in January 2019, my plan was to ask her out once she arrived.

But everything took a wild turn when December hit. Allie told me that she couldn't come to LA in January. This shattered all of my plans. Once again, I was plunged back into the gloom and doom that took hold over my life and I revisited all the lies implanted by the devil concerning how lonely and helpless I was. *I suppose she isn't the one.* I still considered her as someone special and deep inside, I wanted to date her. Yet, I still hadn't met her and ironically, I didn't think long-distance would work. So, I decided to not respond to her messages and slowly cut her off.

ALLIE:

I noticed Barnabas was taking longer to respond to my emails. We went from talking every other day to once a week, maximum. During that time, I also had more free time than usual as I recently left my job. Days would go by and I did not hear back from Barnabas, and when he did respond there seemed to be more distance than before. *I wonder what I did wrong?*

Finally, the emails ceased.

Discouraged and sad, I leaned on my mom as she stroked my hair. "Allie, how is Barnabas doing?" she asked.

To her surprise, I responded, "Don't even mention his name. He stopped responding to me, so I'm not sure what's going on."

She calmly reassured me, "Okay I won't talk about him. But just know that he will come back to you. You are a special girl, Allie."

Her words were drowned out by my doubtful thoughts. *Lord, now how will you fulfill what you told me about him? I thought he was going to be my husband.*

I wrote down two prayers in my journal on December 12th, 2018:

A prayer to Jesus:
My Creator who is seated above earth as His footstool,

I pray that in a year from now, You will continue to transform and shape me. I pray that, in a year from now, I will be totally different, in a good way. My Lord, my hope is in You. My hope isn't in marriage, though I would love to be married. My hope isn't in what my life will become. My hope is in You, Jesus!

One day You will come back and wipe away my tears. Lord, my flesh keeps failing me but I will hope in You, Jesus. Please comfort my lonely heart. Please fill me with your love, peace, and joy. May You allow me to grow tremendously in seasons of waiting. May I grow inpatience and not grow weary of doing what is right. I love You Lord Jesus, so please be with me. I need You, whether I'm happy, sad, empty, or content. I need You regardless.

Please let Your presence be with me right now. Please don't let me fall.

A prayer for Barnabas
Lord Jesus,

I pray you continue to do good works in him. I pray that he walks in your grace and grows in your great love. If he is flying back to Hong Kong, I pray that it will be a smooth flight and he can witness to whomever you place next to him.

What my mom spoke to me eventually proved to be true.

BARNABAS:

A few months passed since I distanced myself from Allie. It was March, and I was once again at the height of my reappearing existential crisis (this is an overdramatic statement. It wasn't that, that bad). But Allie surprised me on my birthday. She requested a video call. In the call, which was during her lunch break, she ran from her office to the shoreline on "Ali'i drive" (we later joke about it being "Allie drive"), showing me the clear and beautiful Hawaiian waters. I was overwhelmed by the beauty while feeling absolutely terrible—because I knew what I had done to her by ignoring her messages and efforts to dialogue.

I thought that conversation was only a one-time thing. But Allie persisted to contact me every day after my birthday. Feeling guilty as well as touched by her kindness, we started video chatting and talking. We would also end in prayer. Every night after our call and prayer, I felt internally conflicted as I remembered the sign that the Lord gave me months ago. Yet, I was also unsure if it would really work out moving forward as we have not once met up in person.

After another two weeks of talking, I finally decided to reveal my cards from the beginning.

Allie:

Barnabas wanted to call. While I had been the one who usually took the initiative to call, I noticed that lately, he had taken the lead. He sent me a message, "Hey, there is something I want to tell you." *Oh no! Am I being pursued by him? Suddenly I'm not sure what to do!*

Barnabas:

I confessed my feelings and my interest in a potential dating relationship. I also clarified why I did what I did in the past months.

Allie:

I was stunned. Quickly I responded, "The feelings are mutual..!"

Barnabas:

That felt super amazing! I had never felt so good in my life. *Yes! Finally!*

Still, we also concluded that we would seek for another sign from the Lord and decided to fast for one week in which we would only eat one meal in a 24-hour interval.

At the end of the week, while I was reading my daily devotions, I came across Psalm 118 and felt extremely prompted to share this psalm with Allie. Before I continue, let me explain how devotions work for me. I follow a concise day-by-day Bible reading plan which allows me to go through every verse of Scripture at least twice a year (I write this not to brag. Rather, my encounter with Christians in China motivated me to pursue Scripture the way they did). In other words, there is a designated and predestinated bunch of Scripture for each day. Thus, it was not by chance that I read Psalm 118 that morning.

We called that evening, and to my surprise, I said something that left Allie in tears . . .

Allie:

Barnabas revealed something to me in order to be open and honest in our relationship. Once he told me, I tried to remain calm by smiling it off. But knowing me, someone who wears their heart on their sleeve, I couldn't conceal my emotions. In a soft, small voice I said, "I'm sorry. I can't. I need to go." The call dropped and I cried, "Is this really Your will, Lord?"

Barnabas:

I was sitting outside the library when the call was cut. I stared into the night feeling empty. I have tried hard in preserving myself for the one whom the Lord has promised me and I really felt that this was special. Not only had I fallen in love with her, I could actually see a future together. We shared the same doctrines, beliefs, and passion for the Gospel. Our personalities matched really well.

We even used the same emojis when we messaged each other and didn't feel awkward about it. Everything felt right.

Thus, after I vulnerably revealed everything, I feared that this would be another major relational disappointment—no different from the past seven years of committing myself to the Lord in singleness. *Oh Lord. Please remember me.*

Allie:

I went into a closet with my Bible and came across Psalm 118, which really resonated with me. After reading the Bible and praying, I told my mom about everything that had just happened. God spoke through her and encouraged me to keep talking with Barnabas and show him grace.

I called Barnabas and poured out my heart to him about my feelings and what my mom had told me. Then, he responded, "We should read Psalm 118 together." As we exchanged turns reading each verse, I suddenly realized that it was the same passage that I had just read.

Barnabas & Allie:

Perhaps it was not in the way that we expected, but the Lord answered our prayer for a sign at the end of our fast—Psalm 118. Looking back, the Lord has given us multiple signs. He had been our matchmaker and brought us together.

He spoke to us individually, gave us Psalm 118 during a difficult time, and even allowed us to find favor with our parents who were supportive of our pursuit of one another. Thus, we began our dating relationship just like that!

Chapter 4

What is Love?

THE NEXT FEW CHAPTERS will explore more deeply into the heavyweight topics of dating, sex, and marriage. All those topics surround one thing—love. Without a basis and explanation of love, we can't meaningfully discuss those other topics. So, what is love?

Some might respond to this topic by going to 1 Corinthians 13:4–8.

> "Love is patient and kind; love does not envy or boast; it is not arrogant or rude. It does not insist on its own way; it is not irritable or resentful; it does not rejoice at wrongdoing, but rejoices with the truth . . . " (13:4–6)

This is indeed a beautiful passage on the topic of love, but it does not define love. This passage describes love; that love is characterized by and visible through patience and kindness. It portrays what one who loves would do, that one would not "envy or boast" nor would one be arrogant or rude. Even if we argue that love is an accumulation of all the qualities in this passage, is love merely defined by these qualities?

Others might respond with a popular phrase: "love is love." While different people may mean differently with this phrase, one possible interpretation is that "love is a recollection of the experiences that has brought forth the feeling of love." In other words, love is whatever that makes me feel loved.

One quick problem that this notion runs into is that it leaves "love" undefined. If "love" is solely based on one's subjective experiences, then how do we differentiate between what's loving and what's not? Surely, not everything is love, right? Hopefully we can all agree that rape, a pedophile's "affection" for an underaged person, or murder isn't loving. But why not?

This is where Scripture sheds wisdom and insight on this massive topic and substance that many people are in search of. Scripture writes: "God is love." (1 John 4:8; 4:16) This doesn't mean that love is god, as God is not an emotion nor just a standard—He is the maximally great Being, the greatest Great. God is also revealed in Three Persons and made Himself personally accessible and knowable, even as a friend (John 15:15).

When Scripture writes: "God is love," the presented idea is similar to Mark 10:18, where Jesus says that "no one is good but God alone." Just as God defines moral goodness in Mark 10:18, that only He is good, God defines love as He is love. This means that love is not only subjective and emotional, but that love is transcendent and objective—love has a standard that is based on God's character and actions. How do we know love? We look at Jesus.

Two Characteristics of Love:

Love characterized by moral goodness.

Here's a simple formula: If A = B and A = C, then B = C. In the same way, if God = moral goodness and God = love, then love = moral goodness—love is morally good. This is why the likes of rape, theft, and murder are not loving, because such actions are not morally good. If we take out the God-given standard of moral goodness from love, we cannot establish any objective and logical consistent notion of love.

The Bible is full of examples, but we'll present a few. Consider 1 Corinthians 13:6, "[love] does not rejoice at wrongdoing, but rejoices with the truth."

There's a lot to unpack here. First, God is the truth and truth is in God (e.g.: John 1:14; 1:17; 8:31-32; 8:44-45; 14:6; 2 Cor 13:8; Gal 5:7; Eph 1:13; 4:21; 2 Tim 2:25). So, when love rejoices with the truth, it signifies that love—or whatever that is loving—rejoices and celebrates with what God celebrates. Second, the word "wrongdoing" is a moralistic word. Love does not rejoice with wrongdoing because God is not a wrongdoer; God only does good as He is good. Romans 12:9-10, "Let love be genuine. Abhor what is evil; hold fast to what is good," present a similar idea.

Consider 1 Timothy 1:5 as well, "The aim of our charge is love that issues from a pure heart and a good conscience and a sincere faith."

In this passage, we see love being associated with three things: (1) purity, (2) good conscience, and (3) a sincere faith. Let's unpack two things. First, a good conscience is defined in Hebrews 13:18 as the desire to act honorably in all things. If we look a little deeper into the context of that passage, it appears that the author of Hebrews was exhorting the church to pray for them, so that they would do honorably and the right thing in God's sight. Second, going back to 1 Timothy 1:5, the word "pure" (*katharos*) is oftentimes translated in Greek as "clean" (cf. Matt 27:59; Lk 11:41; Rom 14:20). The things that are clean are contrasted with those that are *un*clean (*akatharos* cf. Matt 12:43; Mark 1:23; 3:11; 1 Cor 7:14; 2 Cor 6:17). There's a standard of what's clean and unclean, and love is on the pure, honorable, and sincere side of things. Guess what, God is also pure, honorable, and sincere—so sincere that He sent His Son in our place for our sin. So, love is also measured via a standard, a standard based on God.

Love characterized by selflessness and sacrifice

Immediately after 1 John 4:8, the famous "God is love" passage, John continues to write in 1 John 4:9-10 (cf. John 3:16):

> "In this the love of God was made manifest among us, that God sent his only Son into the world, so that we might live through Him."

The love of God is characterized by the sending of Jesus Christ, with the result that we would live and not die through Him. God sending His son is selfless and self-sacrificial, and the result of the recipients, that we are able to live, is for our benefit. Romans 5:8 writes similarly: "but God shows his love for us in that while we were still sinners, Christ died for us."

If this was a little confusing, don't worry! A few examples should clear it up:

Example 1: Loving God

Jesus says that the greatest commandment is to love God with everything (e.g.: Matt 22:36–37). This certainly involves our emotion and heart, perhaps even shouting in worship, "I love you, Jesus!" However, it also involves a standard as Jesus says, "If anyone loves Me, he will keep My word." (John 14:23; 14:15; 14:21; 15:10; 1 John 5:3; 2 John 1:6 cf. Deut 6:1–6). The keeping of God's Word presents a standard. In other words, how we know whether or not we truly love God is by how much we keep His word, similar to how a citizen who loves the king will gladly obey the king's laws.

Consider 1 John 4:20 (cf. John 13:35; 1 John 2:4; 2:9; 4:12) which writes:

> "If anyone says, "I love God," and hates his brother, he is a liar; for he who does not love his brother whom he has seen cannot love God whom he has not seen."

The logic is simple. Since Scripture tells us to love one another, one who loves God will love one another. If one doesn't love but hates the other, even if he/she claims to love God, this person does not truly love God—"he is a liar."

As for the aspect of selflessness and self-sacrifice, when Jesus says, "But seek first the kingdom of God and His righteousness, and all these things will be added to you," (Matt 6:33) He is telling us to not seek first the things for ourselves. Rather, He's telling us to put God and His Kingdom first and to be selfless and self-sacrificial since it's not about us anyway. Luke presents something even more intense: "If anyone would come after me, let him deny himself and take up his cross daily and follow me." (Lk 9:23 cf. 14:27) To love God, which is to keep His word, involves carrying our crosses daily in following Him.

Example 2: Loving Others

The second greatest commandment is "love your neighbor as yourself" (e.g.: Matt 22:37), in which Jesus says that His disciples will be known by their love for one another (John 13:35). Again, loving one another isn't about letting one have their way, but also points to a standard. Consider Galatians 5:14 (cf. Matt 7:14; 22:40; Rom 13:8–10; Jas 2:8), "For the whole law is fulfilled in one word: 'You shall love your neighbor as yourself.'"

The mentioning of the Mosaic Law should immediately draw your attention to an objective standard. The law generally presents a standard as one either keeps it or breaks it. Galatians 5:14 is indicating that loving one's neighbor should be done objectively according to what the Law says.

Looking back at Matthew 22:39, which writes: "And a second is like it: You shall love your neighbor as yourself," this passage does not indicate self-love, or "love your neighbor in the way you love yourself." Rather, Jesus commands us to love our neighbors according to the Mosaic Law, which applies even to "yourself" as it is objective. Let that sink in. Jesus cites this passage from Leviticus 19:18, perhaps from the most boring book of the Bible as it's all Law; and guess what, Jesus quotes this verse to a Pharisaic lawyer (22:34–35). Would they have interpreted this passage as "I love you in the way I love me," or "I (am commanded to) love you and me because God loves us—and this is revealed in His Word (Law)"? The fact that Matthew 22:40 writes, "On these two commandments depend all the Law and the Prophets," shows that the second greatest commandment does not present a love that is subjective, but one that is objective, as per a standard set by God in accordance to who He is.

As for the aspect of selflessness and self-sacrifice in loving one another, this notion cannot be clearer in Scripture. Galatians 5:13 writes: " . . . but through love serve one another." Offering service to one another is selfless—it is for the benefit of others on behalf of our own labor and effort. Consider one more passage, John 15:12–13:

> "This is my commandment, that you love one another as I have loved you. Greater love has no one than this, that someone lay down his life for his friends."

Isn't this clear? Jesus tells us that a greater form of love for one another is self-sacrifice—which God Himself ultimately demonstrates.

So, what is love? God is love. Love is characterized by Him—by His standard of goodness and by His example of love, displayed through His selflessness and ultimate self-sacrifice. While love can be expressed in various ways, true love will always be categorized by the two basic features mentioned above. More examples of love in our love story will follow.

Chapter 5

First Encounter—Kona

BARNABAS & ALLIE:
Perhaps ironically, one of the first topics we talked about was physical and sexual intimacy. It's ironic because there was no physical touch nor intimacy—though we were experiencing tons of spiritual and emotional intimacy. Even though there were no plans for when we would meet up for the first time, sex was out of the question until we got married. We even agreed that we wouldn't kiss until the day of our wedding.

You might wonder why we decided to not have sex nor kiss before marriage. More about sex will be explored in chapter 7, but in short, we didn't think that it was loving (now that there is a definition of love) to engage in those activities as a dating couple. Would it be loving—morally good and selfless—if we had sex and Barnabas got Allie pregnant? Even if she didn't get pregnant, would it be loving for us to have sex and then venture on separate locations during our upcoming long-distance relationship?

As for the issue of kissing, while different believers have different convictions on this issue, it proved to be a slippery slope for us. Barnabas certainly envisioned himself treading down the paths of sexual urge and desire for Allie if he had kissed and made-out with her. This would then lead back to the issue of whether or not such an action was loving.

Barnabas:

It was the middle of March and we have been talking and interacting as a dating couple for a week. Our souls were being drawn to each together closer and closer. Yet, something was still off, that is, I still hadn't met Allie. I found her tremendously attractive, beautiful, and cute, but I didn't really know what she really looked like in person. This bothered me.

On a Sunday afternoon after church, I decided that I had to visit her. Our tentative plan by then was to meet during summer, after I was done with my Junior year. But I couldn't wait; and mind you, no one on this planet knew about this relationship aside from our parents.

I hurriedly looked up tickets to Kona and surprisingly found an affordable round-trip ticket that could somehow fit into my hectic semester. I immediately asked her if I could visit within one week's notice, and not only did she say "yes," her family gave me their approval as well. I also immediately asked my parents if they would allow me to do something that is out of my character—as I am a planner (I usually plan my flights at least six months in advance)—and somehow, they also approved of this trip.

I was so excited and so scared. The fact that I would be leaving for a week meant that I had to skip classes while completing all my assignments, projects, and work beforehand. During the last four days before my departure, I fasted and ate one meal in 24-hour intervals because there was no way I could accomplish everything on my own strength. I desperately needed God's help and wisdom, and He generously allowed me to complete everything before I left. I was able to leave for Hawaii to meet my girl without the worries of school and work. Hallelujah!

First Encounter — Kona

Allie:

Interestingly, my family and I were on vacation when all this took place, so I was in Texas when I received Barnabas's message requesting to visit me in a few days. *Oh no.* My mom was shocked. "As soon as we return home, we have to clean the house!" she said. And it was true. Once we arrived back in Kona, there was only a day and a half until Barnabas arrived. Panicked, I dusted and vacuumed every inch of my room and scrubbed the shower until it was sparkling clean.

Barnabas was arriving the next day.

Day 1: Thursday

Allie:

It was 4:45pm. 15 minutes until I got off from work, and two hours until I met Barnabas for the first time. Suddenly, my excitement turned into fear. *Oh no, this can't be happening! I don't even know this guy. What have I done? I hope his flight gets cancelled. Ugh, it's too late! He is on his way, there is no turning back.* At this point, I didn't even know his height, and somehow, I thought he was much shorter than me.

Barnabas:

On the six-hour flight to Kona, I spent half the time grading papers and the other half feeling as if I was the dumbest person on earth. *What on earth am I doing? I don't even know her.* I suddenly remembered my mom's cautious advice, that I should book a hotel with free cancellation just in case something didn't work out. *I really should've done that.* I tried reassuring myself that, even if this didn't work out, I could at least try to minister to her family. *Well, it is what it is.*

My flight landed around 7pm in Kona, and I was going to meet her anytime.

Allie:

I arrived at the airport and waited near the domestic arrivals. The airport was outdoors and the only thing that separated the arrival hall from the baggage claim were automatic sliding doors. Every time the door opened, I thought it would be Barnabas. Finally, after multiple rounds of pacing back-and-forth, hoping to enthusiastically approach my "boyfriend," I got tired.

Then I saw him.

I ran up to give him a hug and wrapped a lei around his neck as per Hawaiian customs.

Barnabas:

I froze when Allie approached me, hugged me, and put a beautiful lei around my neck. *Wait what? She's Allie? She's shorter than I thought!* I was shocked because I assumed that I would pick up my luggage before meeting her. This way, I could have some more time to be mentally prepared to meet her.

Allie:

We were both unprepared to meet each other. While waiting for his luggage, we awkwardly snapped a photo together. We then silently walked to my car.

While driving home, I had no idea what to say. I blasted worship music to tune out the tension and awkwardness of driving this "stranger" home. As the silence began to creep in even more, Barnabas asked, "Hey, has your opinion of me changed after meeting in person?" This sudden comment snapped me back into reality. I quickly tried to reassure him, "No, no . . . Of course not . . . " but internally, I was thinking: *"Oh no! We both seem awkward. This is weird. Is he really the one that I'm going to marry?"* Such internal turbulence made me feel like I was back on a flight again—one which I wasn't enjoying at all. Yet, I felt God say in that moment: "Just wait and have grace. Have grace."

Barnabas:

Within half-an-hour of meeting my girlfriend, whom I almost didn't recognize at first as she was a lot cuter than I thought, I met her parents too! Boy, that was stressful. Yet, they were welcoming, kind, and generous—and I had the best food of my life during that week with them.

Allie:

We were at the dinner table and I wasn't making any effort in engaging with my "boyfriend." *Wow, he's my boyfriend, and yet I don't really know him.* Again, God suddenly filled me with compassion. I realized that he probably didn't know what was happening either and I should act like a good host as if he was an exchange student.

Barnabas:

As we sat at the table stacked with all kinds of good food: somen salad, chicken katsu, sushi, mint chocolate cake, and ice cream for dinner. I didn't eat much as I was nervous. What was funny was that I came from fasting and didn't eat anything on the flight, so I was very hungry. Looking back, I really wished I had eaten more that night.

Allie:

Once dinner ended, I showed him the room that he would be staying in—my room, in which I spent hours cleaning and clearing out drawers! Where did I sleep? Smack middle in the living room without AC. If it wasn't for my mom, who made me clear out my drawers and stuff my clothes in their closet, I really wouldn't have done it.

    Sitting on the floor of my room, I said, "Hey, why don't we do some worship together?" Barnabas agreed and picked up the guitar. We started worshiping together. The moment we began to worship, everything fell back into place. The awkward tension, the nervousness, and the doubts melted away.

Once worship ended, we talked with ease in the way that we would normally converse on the phone. Everything just clicked. I pulled out my camera and began snapping a few photos of him. With new lenses, I realized that he was pretty good-looking.

Barnabas:

We couldn't talk for too long as Allie had work the next day. I checked out the bed that I would be sleeping on. On the pillow, Allie left me a cute gift bag containing: a letter, pen, hand-drawn picture of both of us, anointing prayer oil, and soap. At the edge of the bed, there was a large container containing a wash towel, toothbrush, sunscreen, aloe cream for sunburns and a small facial towel.

"Ding." I checked my phone. Allie had sent me the Wi-Fi password to their place and told me that she even left a bottle of water outside my room. At this moment, I was tearing up and overwhelmingly touched by her hospitality and kindness. I do not know what I have done to earn their love and generosity. The level of care shown to me exceeded that of a five-star hotel, and I remembered the most consistent word that my mother spoke to me about my future wife for the past four years, "the woman whom the Lord joins you to will exceed your expectations." Allie had truly exceeded all my expectations and shown me a love that was far greater than what I expected and deserved.

Then I showered in a foreign bathroom using Allie's pink and girly body wash and shampoo. That was certainly an experience.

Barnabas & Allie:

Looking back, this experience was rather ironic because until we met, Allie was all-in with confidence, yet filled with doubt and insecurity once we encountered each other. On the other hand, Barnabas was filled with doubt and worries until he met Allie.

FIRST ENCOUNTER—KONA

Day 2: Friday
Barnabas:

This was one of the most adventurous days of my life. Almost the entire day, Uncle David, Allie's dad, took me out on a road trip across the Big Island of Hawaii! Not only was this my first road trip in Hawaii, it was also my first road trip in the States—just me, him, and nature.

Though it was nerve-wracking in the beginning as I had to interact with my girlfriend's dad alone for around eight hours, it became a truly memorable and amazing experience. Uncle David took me to Punalu'u Beach (black sand beach), volcano national park, and Akaka Falls. Not only did he drive the entire time, as I didn't have my license yet, he also treated me to wonderful Kona coffee and lunch. During lunch at the volcano national park, he sent me off and told me to call Allie—as she was on her lunch break too. We talked while I walked around seeing lava and other scenes that I had never seen before. I will forever remember the love and kindness that he showed me that day. I take none of it for granted, especially when he had just met me.

Above all, I believe we truly bonded through our conversations. We talked pretty much the entire time together, again, around eight hours total. To this day, Allie and I don't talk for eight hours straight on our road trips. We eat and listen to music, books, and sermons. But in those eight hours together with my future father-in-law, he told me everything, including the fact that Allie wanted to get married to me! What a pleasant and unexpected surprise. He even told me unheard stories of Allie and that she was a very sweet girl.

She is a very sweet girl.

Allie:

That night, we had our first date. This is how it went down: I drove home from work and hurriedly did my make-up. Somehow, I was very nervous, and the eyeliner got into my eye. Here I was, crying with messed up make-up, trying to get ready for my first date with Barnabas. He called and said he was only 20 minutes away. *Ugh! I look like a hot mess!*

We decided to go to a popular seafood restaurant. Once we arrived, we found the parking lot to be quite full. It was pretty dark and a bit sketchy. Suddenly, Barnabas grabbed my wrist. I thought: *"What? Is he trying to hold my hand? Why is he grabbing my wrist?"* We walked to the restaurant wrist-in-hand.

Barnabas:

I just wanted to hold her hand, but I didn't know how to, so I ended up grabbing her wrist. She confronted me about it and taught me how to hold her hand properly. That proved to be a valuable and sweet lesson.

Anyway, we realized that the wait time was relatively long, so Allie took us somewhere else.

Allie:

In the trunk of my car, I stored fairy lights and a long beach towel for a night picnic. We made a quick stop at an undisclosed sandwich place and proceeded to our secret destination.

On the way, I had little to say, so, Barnabas scrambled to lighten up the mood with some cheesy jokes. They weren't funny, but I chuckled a little. Finally, we arrived at a pitch-black remote area. I set up the string lights and laid down the towels.

Barnabas:

That was scary. Raised in Hong Kong, I was used to endless bright lights. Yet, here I was in the middle of an island with no lights. I could even uninvitedly see the stars and worried that someone would secretly attack us. Thankfully, nothing bad happened that night.

As we settled down and started talking, everything felt normal again. Allie began to open up and share some of her of feelings and fears. I tried to respond in the most loving and caring way possible. We ended up bonding well. Interestingly, unlike most first dates where couples only tread on shallow waters, ours was a scuba dive that hit the depths of the ocean. Though it might have not been conventional, our relationship had never been so in the first place.

Thus, we ended our first date with cheerful spirits and slowly climbed to cloud nine in our remaining time together.

Day 3-4: Saturday & Sunday
Barnabas & Allie:

We had tons of memorable moments—memories that played a huge role in keeping us tight-knit as we were about to embark on our long-distance relationship. Every morning, we would begin our day with worship. This was one of our ways of purposefully placing God at the center of our relationship before doing anything else. After all, it was all His work that led us together.

Barnabas:

While Allie was driving us to the beach, she saw a person holding a sign requesting food. Without a second thought, she drove to the nearest supermarket and bought food and water for that man. Not only did we deliver him food, she even prayed and shared the Gospel with him. I was shocked by her boldness and Kingdom-mindedness—even on our first whole day together! Wow, God had truly given me a partner who loved Him.

Allie:

It was Barnabas's first time experiencing tumbling waves. At one point, I told him that I'll hold his hand and never let go—only to find him getting smashed by the waves and tumbling to a different island (yes, this is an exaggeration). We decided to change plans. I thought using tubes would help him. As we both started blowing the tubes, I realized that by the time I finished, his tube was limply deflated. I told myself, "*I guess it's because he's a tourist. Maybe he doesn't experience these things like I do.*" I waited another ten minutes for him to inflate his tube.

Barnabas:

Even though it was rather embarrassing and stressful for me to blow up the tube (it was my first time!), I still had tons of fun that day. In fact, that was probably the first time I've enjoyed swimming and hanging out at a beach.

That evening, Uncle David made fresh poke for us. It was the best poke I've ever had in my life! The fish was refreshing, as it was alive only hours ago. Aunty Faith also took us out to a local store and bought us memorable gifts. I felt deeply loved and accepted by the Yamakawa family.

Allie:

The next morning, we woke at 5am as I wanted to begin our day with worship at the beach. It was still dark when we headed out. I took him to the same beach as the first date night—though Barnabas didn't know.

The road was still closed since parking didn't open until later. We decided to walk down the road to Kua Bay. For the entire time, Barnabas carried the guitar down the steep, rocky, swerving road. It was beautiful. The sky was a light blue color sprinkled with ripened orange streaks. We then had a sweet time of worship while engaging with God in His gorgeous creation.

Barnabas:

As we walked back to the car with my arms aching, though I pretended the guitar wasn't heavy at all, we talked about our future wedding plans. In that conversation, my presupposed plans to get married in a grand wedding—as I've witnessed in Hong Kong—slowly began to change.

Allie:

As much as I've admired weddings, I've had the mindset that it's only one day. It's a very special day, but ultimately, that one day is meant for a lifetime. My parents only had two witnesses at their wedding. My sister also had a small wedding only with her immediate family. This background shaped my perspective as I witnessed my parents being married for 30 years and onwards. I just wanted to get married to Barnabas, regardless of the size of the wedding. As long as we could be together, I would be happy.

Barnabas:

Allie was right. We didn't have to get married in a grand wedding with 500 people, 1000 lights, and 2000 flowers. Don't get me wrong, there's nothing wrong with those and that was still the only thing I associated with weddings at that point. But if anything, a wedding points to a marriage, and a grand wedding doesn't necessarily guarantee a grand, long-lasting marriage. I wanted a successful marriage with my wife that testifies of God's greatness and truthfulness.

After attending church, I met up with some of Allie's friends from high school. During lunch, I was stressed because I felt like a complete stranger—even to Allie. She was a whole different person. I saw her amazing leadership and communication skills. I could tell that she was adored and respected by her peers. I was so proud of my girl.

Day 5: Monday

Barnabas:

This was the last day before my departure back to the reality of college. While Allie was at work, I was busy grading and catching up with upcoming assignments. It was as if my feet were slowly dipping back into the pool of endless stress. Hawaii did feel like paradise, as I was able to fully detach myself from my daily routines and enjoy a nice week-long sabbatical with my girlfriend.

That afternoon, Uncle David took me to meet Allie during lunch. We met at a small café and officially announced our relationship. We announced our relationship on the first of April . . . and it certainly made a scene as many people were unsure of whether our relationship was real.

Allie:

For dinner, we went to a steakhouse with my parents. My mom predicted that we would get married by the end of the year. My dad, not wanting to make us uncomfortable, hinted at my mom to not talk about it for now. The thought of marrying Barnabas at the end of the year seemed unlikely. I couldn't imagine being married to him in eight months.

After dinner, we drove to a beach near my house. I felt a pang of sorrow as I knew this was our last night together. We didn't know when we would meet again as Barnabas would soon go back to Hong Kong, making it a lot more difficult to communicate regularly. We sat on the edge of a rocky wall with our feet dangling over the ocean. I opened up to Barnabas more about some things that have happened to me in the past and how they impacted me. Regardless, I let him know that I was still a new creation in Christ.

I stood up and dusted my knees. Barnabas remained on the rock wall, but this time, he knelt down, took my hands in his, and prayed for me. Tears welled up. He made me feel like a princess, one who is safely cherished and loved by the King.

Barnabas:

When we got home later that evening, I asked Allie to sit down on the couch while I hurriedly brought in a gigantic bucket from their garden. I began to wash the bucket while Allie watched in confusion and curiosity. She looked like a little puppy as she continued to stare at me, not knowing what would happen. After washing the bucket, I filled it with warm water and placed it in front of her. I then took out my Bible and read to her John 13:1–20, the passage where Jesus washed His disciples' feet.

Allie began to tear up as she figured out what I was going to do. She said, "If you wash my feet, I wash your feet." I replied saying: "You sound like someone from that passage (wink)." This got the job done. I then proceeded to wash her feet as she was filled with emotion. She said: "No one has ever done this for me!"

Day 6: Tuesday

Barnabas:

It was around 6:30 in the morning and Allie was waiting outside my door. Once I was awake, she wanted to worship and we sang a few quick songs. In the most anti-climactic manner, we said our goodbyes as she headed off to work. After a while, Uncle David took me to the airport and I was on my flight back to reality.

On the flight, I ate the dorayaki (red bean pancake) that Allie made for me while re-watching all the videos we recorded together. Every bite was accompanied with falling teardrops. For the next four months, these videos were the only memories we had together in person.

Chapter 6

Second Encounter—Hong Kong

BARNABAS & ALLIE:

A lot has happened since our first encounter in Kona. Barnabas completed his junior year of college and returned to Hong Kong for a busy summer, working multiple jobs, while Allie remained steadfastly in her hometown. Not only was there an 18-hour time difference that hindered communication, Barnabas also had a limited internet phone plan that rendered video call impossible unless he was at home. Sadly, Barnabas was rarely at home due to work. Furthermore, Hong Kong is a densely populated city. There's hardly anywhere, aside from one's home, where one can be alone. Thus, our communication was always interrupted by a plethora of ongoing noises.

On Allie's end, summer felt slower than usual. She began a new job which required her to wake up at 5am every morning. As she drove to work, we would try to squeeze in a quick call. By the time she started work, Barnabas was fast asleep. Life was, again, routine and boring.

Still, we were able to set a date in August to meet in Hong Kong. This encounter marked a lot of growth and surprises in our relationship, as we finally reunited after four months of difficult long-distance dating—one of which was our engagement.

Our Encounter in Hong Kong

Allie:

It was finally the long-awaited day to meet Barnabas. Sadly, it was really a long wait as I had to wait for another two hours on the plane doing nothing. I remembered everyone was screaming in Cantonese. I had to ask someone who sat next to me about why everyone else was loud and annoyed. She angrily yelled: "Our flight is delayed!" This was only a first taste of what my trip would eventually look like.

I finally arrived at the airport to be greeted with a bouquet of white roses with pink tips. Barnabas and I were super awkward. We filled our conversations with "yay" and "wow" as we didn't quite know what to say or how to interact again. It almost felt worse and more unnatural than our first encounter.

Hong Kong was also a lot different from Kona. It was filled with skyscrapers with narrowly packed roads. It was also the first place where I truly felt like a foreigner.

Barnabas & Allie:

Things didn't stay awkward for too long. It took us around 3 days to get used to each other again, and everything was fine. We explored Hong Kong during our first week there. We went to amusement parks, met with both sides of Barnabas's extended family, and tried out all kinds of Cantonese delicacies. Barnabas's parents, family, and friends generously treated us to lots of good food as well. We were practically together every day and safely guarded every special moment we had with each other. For Barnabas, this was a dream-come-true. He could finally show his hometown to his girl.

Allie:

And it was true. I saw another side of Barnabas. Instead of the meek and nervous Barnabas I first met in Kona, I witnessed a confident and assertive Barnabas. For a good amount of my time there, I was sick. Barnabas was adamant about me taking medication exactly every 4 hours as the doctor prescribed. The most distinct time was when we were at a cute and cozy cafe. I had ordered a macchiato and chocolate cake. I hear Barnabas shuffling through his bag only to pull out all my prescribed medication. "Come on Allie, it's been 4 hours. Time to take your medication." *He's going to make do this even in a cafe?* Little did I know, his care and concern for my body and health became a constant theme after we got married.

Barnabas:

One iconic moment that we shared in Hong Kong, before being engaged, was a talk with my pastor, pastor Ken. We will forever remember that conversation. Without disclosing personal details, we were both weeping (actually weeping) near the end of the conversation as we were overwhelmingly touched by his example in marriage. The pastor's story of demonstrating selfless and unconditional love struck us to our core. He even gave me one of his books that taught him what marital love was. If anything, this conversation taught us perseverance—something that we needed a lot in the days to come.

What was interesting about that conversation was its timing. We were committed to marriage and talked about our eventual wedding date immediately at a cafe after our meeting with the pastor. By then, our tentative plan of marriage date was set to be around three years. Yet, God had a different plan—one that was sooner and unpredictable.

Barnabas and Allie:

Looking back, we believed God orchestrated our conversation with pastor Ken to foreshadow our upcoming marriage and to prepare us, similar to a premarital counseling session, for what was to come. We did other premarital counseling activities, but this one trumped everything else.

Second Encounter—Hong Kong

The Proposal Story

Barnabas:

Logistically, I thought about getting married after I graduated with my master's degree because it would benefit us, both in our careers and finances. Thus, the thought of proposing to her did not come to mind at all.

Yet, all my plans collapsed on the evening of August 15th. The more I have come to know the Lord, the more I realized that His will is truly far better and far more complex than mine. That night, we were walking along the shoreline of Victoria Harbor, gazing at the notorious Hong Kong skyline.

As we walked and saw the beautiful night lights, I began to shed tears. Yesterday afternoon at the cafe after meeting pastor Ken, we talked about pushing forward our marriage plans. We decided that we would try to get married within two years. That actually bothered me. It wasn't the person I was marrying that proved to be a problem—Allie was amazing, and I loved her with all my heart. I couldn't wait to marry her. However, I was rather worried for my parents. They had been there for me all my life. At times, they were the only ones who knew me and stood by my side, especially through all the times I had to switch schools and adapt to a new environment. We would even call almost every day during my college years, and my parents would constantly leave me tons of supportive and encouraging messages in our group chat. *What would happen to my parents if I married Allie? How could I care and support them as their only child if we ended up living somewhere else?* The fact that they were aging didn't help my fears and burdens and Hong Kong had one of the highest costs of living in the world.

In the midst of such a heavy burden, Allie took me to a nearby coffee shop that faced the skyline. Noticing the heaviness in my heart, she re-expressed her desire to follow me to the ends of the earth—to wherever the Lord calls us to be. She also told me that she would wait for the right time for us to get married, regardless of how long it might take.

I was filled with love and gratitude. Once we arrived back home, I told Allie to stay in her room as I frantically discussed with my parents about proposing to her the next day. Even though they had only met my girlfriend for a week, they loved her and testified that they had never seen me this happy. Thus, they approved my proposal request but asked about my plan. I told them that I had no plan whatsoever. I had no ring nor a location, but I had faith. Naively, I believed that if this was truly His will, He would make a way as He did throughout our relationship. I went to sleep just like that.

Allie:

I knew something was fishy when Barnabas told me to leave my room, after first telling me to stay in my room. *Why did he have me leave my room? What is he talking about with his parents in Cantonese?* Normally, he would plainly speak in English, even with his parents, to make me feel more included in the conversation. He would rarely speak Cantonese unless he had to. Something just didn't add up.

Barnabas:

Then came August 16th, two days before Allie's departure. Waking up with a hopeful spirit, I immediately messaged my close friends in Hong Kong regarding where to get a ring. I hadn't considered proposing to the extent that I didn't even know where to buy a wedding ring. Since these messages were sent during the summer heat, I feared that they wouldn't respond, as even I wouldn't wake up early in the morning unless there was some sort of appointment. Yet, to my surprise, they responded instantly and mentioned the same exact store. I started to think that God truly had something in store for me that day.

Still, I had to consider a way to buy the ring without appearing suspicious. But once I looked up where the store was located, I found out that it was nearby where I lived. Thus, I used the excuse that I would get groceries and then left. I also secretly stole one of the plastic rings that my mom had bought for Allie days ago, when they were having a future mother and daughter in-law bonding moment. This ring was critical in helping me get the right ring size for Allie.

I knew exactly which ring to buy and left the store within five minutes. The best part was that I even got groceries. My alibi was a complete success!

Allie:

Barnabas suddenly told me that he was leaving for the grocery store. I was confused. *Why won't he invite me to the grocery store with him when we normally do everything together?* My suspicion grew larger. *Is he going to buy me a ring? No, Allie! Don't give yourself false hopes.*

I kept questioning Barnabas; "So, Barnabas, what were you talking about last night with your mom? Why did you make me leave my room? Why are you going to the grocery store? Are you going to buy me something too?" I felt his annoyance. We even have videos recording my pestering questions—only for him to react by turning away suspiciously and nervously laughing.

But once I asked him if I should paint my nails and whether I could come with him to get groceries, in which he replied "no" to my nails and "yes" to accompanying him, I lost all hope again. *Well, I suppose he really is getting groceries. Sigh.*

Barnabas:

Initially, I was planning to propose to Allie at Repulse Bay. That idea got repulsed by my parents for good reasons. Instead, they advised me to go to Ma-Wan Beach. At that point, my plan was to arrive there around 4pm and walk around as if nothing was going to happen. My parents, on the other hand, would arrive 30 minutes later with their camera to record the entire scene. Once I took note of their arrival, I would proceed with my proposal. One thing I worried about Ma-Wan beach was that it was relatively popular, especially on Friday afternoons.

Still, I took a step of faith and boarded the taxi to the beach. Strangely enough, as we drove through an iconic bridge in Hong Kong, we were suddenly hit by a massive thunderstorm. We could barely see the road ahead of us. In that moment, instead of being filled with fear and disappointment, I felt a huge wave of peace, as if the Lord was moving in and through the storm. I even teared up a little.

It was once we arrived where I felt one of God's most amazing signs in administering our love story. Not only did the thunderstorm clear the sky, it cleared up the people on the beach as well. God had set the stage for my act.

Allie:

Barnabas told me to get dressed because we're going out. He tried to match my outfit. This was suspicion number three. Anyway, I felt the Lord told me to bring the seashells that I brought all the way from Kona. That was pretty strange, but I listened in obedience.

In the taxi, Barnabas was really serious-looking. His face was like a cold stone. I was still very confused, and when I saw the thunderstorm, I got scared. Looking over at Barnabas, he had tears in his eyes. Was he really so afraid of thunderstorms?

Still, we ended up safely arriving at the beach. After we walked for a bit, I felt prompted to give Barnabas the seashells. Actually, I had no idea that we were going to the beach as Barnabas told me nothing about where we were going. I found that to be funny.

Barnabas:

As I saw the beautiful shells lying on my palm, I knew this was from the Lord. There was truly no turning back. Even right before I was about to propose, the Lord strengthened me with the seashells by the seashore. The Lord had orchestrated everything—and it only gets better!

I then told Allie that I had to use the bathroom. There, I carefully took out the ring box, sliding it into my pocket. At that moment, I just remembered that it might be a good idea to ask for her parents' permission. I knew that the chances of them picking up were slim as there was an 18-hour time difference. While it was Friday, 5:15pm in the Hong Kong afternoon, it was Thursday, 11:15pm in the Hawaiian evening. They could be asleep. However, she responded immediately to my message, "We are free now! You can call us."

I called, and both Mr. and Mrs. Yamakawa were present. That was also a surprise. I told them that I was going to propose to their lovely daughter, Allie. They both responded, first by Aunty Faith followed by Uncle David, "You have our blessing." The Lord had indeed given me success and set the stage to perfection.

Allie:

Barnabas was in the bathroom for a long time. I was getting bored and began shuffling my feet back-and-forth as I walked around the empty beach. He finally came out. He took my hands and led me to walk with him along the shore. He then came to a stop and stood right in front of me. He began his speech. I was frozen when he said: "Well, this is the last day we'll be dating."

"What! Are you breaking up with me?"

He got down on his knees and pulled out the ring. He asked: "Will you marry me?"

Barnabas:

She said "yes" in the most normal tone. It didn't even take her a second to think, as if it was an automated response. Two seconds later, it was as if everything clicked in her mind. She started mumbling, saying words like "what! What! WHAT! I can't believe it!"

Then my parents popped out from the trees and congratulated us while showing us the photos.

Allie:

I called my parents and I was choking up with emotions. I ran into the distance with joy yelling: "I'm getting married to Barnabas!" We ended up eating at a lovely German restaurant facing the beach where we got engaged. As we began eating and talking, he revealed everything that had happened, and I was shocked at how things unfolded by God's grace and power. However, my instinct proved to be accurate, as I knew something fishy was going on in the past 24 hours.

Barnabas and Allie:

Thus, our dating relationship ended, and we became an engaged couple. Once again, God stayed true to His word regarding our relationship.

Chapter 7

Engagement

BARNABAS:

After one full day of being engaged, I sadly escorted my fiancée to the airport early in the morning. I couldn't even linger on the sadness of not having her around as I had my tutoring job immediately that afternoon. To make matters worse, I could not even enter the airport nor carry her luggage to the check-in counter due to some special restrictions that took place in Hong Kong during that season.

I waved her goodbye as I saw the love of my life walk off into the midst of a large airport crowd, again, not knowing when I would see her again.

ALLIE:

I kept crying and crying as Barnabas took me to the airport. I couldn't imagine going back to my routine and boring life without him. I didn't even want to think about waking up at 5am in the morning and only connecting with Barnabas through phone calls and text. We reached the airport and we said our goodbyes. At that time, Barnabas could not accompany me inside the airport for check-in. Exasperated, I sluggishly walked with my two large suitcases to the check-in counter. In fact, where was my counter?

I asked someone if they knew where my counter was. They didn't speak much English but gestured to me to follow them. There I was, all alone in one of the biggest airports I've been to in my life. Barnabas urged me to get some food. I called him, saying: "I can't eat. I'm too sad." He replied: "Allie, you live for Jesus, not me." I was shocked! He put me back in place. I was struck by his words and remembered: *"Oh yes, this life is not for people or relationships, but God!"*

Still, on my transit flight to the Philippines, I could only remain crying alone in my seat. The next ten-hour flight ended up being a long one. I recorded in my journal on August 17, 2020:

> Today I was so sad. I had to say my goodbyes to Barnabas and his family. My heart hurt so much, and my tears were endless. But from weariness You gave me rest. From anxiousness You gave me peace. From loneliness You gave me comfort. I am in awe of You, Jesus. What an amazing Lord I serve. I have no words to say but thank you:
>
> Thank you for knowing me even before I was in my mother's womb.
> Thank you for protecting me all these years. Thank you for being the provider even when I didn't know You.
> Thank you for dying on the cross for my sins.
> Thank you for allowing me to pray to You.
> Thank you for allowing me to cast my burdens on to You.
> Thank you for joining Barnabas and I.

BARNABAS:

Our hearts were even more tight-knit after being engaged. The prospect of getting married a year later felt like forever, and we were looking into the possibility of getting married earlier, though it didn't seem to make sense. While we weren't able to confirm anything nor set a date, I did experience a few distinct instances which, when I looked back, foreshadowed my upcoming wedding and timely marriage.

First, I had a touching farewell with my wonderful small group (or "life group," "kingdom group," "community group," or whatever you call them) at my home church in Hong Kong. They were so kind and faithful to me, even though I could only fellowship with them for less than two months every year. I remembered how they took the time to lay hands and pray for my relationship and future marriage with Allie.

Second, two days before I scheduled to head back to the States for my senior year of college, I was able to meet up with many of my high school friends whom I have not met altogether for years. They all came out to play soccer with me, and afterwards, I was able to share to them how Allie and I got engaged. We had lots of fun and I felt very loved. It was truly a heart-warming event. They treated me that night, saying that it was a gift for my wedding. In terms of monetary value, their gift wasn't much, but the significance and memory behind it was invaluable.

Third, the night before my departure back to the States, I felt compelled to write two emotional letters to my parents. I thanked them for who they are and all that they've done for me in the past. I don't know why I was blessed to be born under their covering and steadfast kindness, and all I can do is give God glory.

As we headed off to the airport the next day, I gave my parents their respective letters and it brought them tears. We probably talked about a lot of things on the way, but one thing that my dad said was: "You'll get married at the end of this year." I suppose the only response I gave him was: "We'll see." Well, this proved to be true.

Setting the Wedding Date

Allie:

It was the last day of August—exactly two weeks after getting engaged. Barnabas already began school and I was back at my 6AM-3PM job. Stumped about the wedding dates, questions filled my mind. *Should we get married during his winter break in a few months? Should we get married after he graduates in two semesters? I don't know.* What I did know was that I wanted to get married to Barnabas soon. With my heart heavily pounding with anxiety, I began to highlight every verse in Psalms about trusting God. Soon, the pages almost looked like a coloring book. I scribbled down a prayer that ended up being pages long, asking for God's will and satisfaction in His timing. At the end of praying, I still felt like the date was late December or early January. *Is this my own desires, or is this God's will?*

Barnabas:

I don't think I've ever felt such an internal division between my heart and mind. Realistically, getting married during Christmas or New Year's would pose many challenges. It would really be a leap of faith, as we would have to fully trust God regarding our future, embracing the unknown—unknown lodging place, unknown job for Allie, unknown vehicle (I didn't own a car at that point), unknown wedding venue and so on. As a thinker and planner, having such incalculable odds should convince me to opt for a different plan.

But I really wanted to get married to her that Christmas break. We both experienced an inner urge and intensity to be married soon. At that point, I felt like my dad supported whatever we decided to do. My mom, on the other hand, had her rightful concerns. Yet, on that same fateful night, she called me and said that, after fasting, she felt a strong sense of peace and encouraged us to get married during that Christmas break.

Barnabas & Allie:

We then set the date for January 3rd, 2020 in Allie's hometown, Kona. With little time to spare, we decided to divide up the work according to our respective locations. Allie would primarily take

Engagement

care of all the work related to the wedding in Kona, while Barnabas would prepare for the issues relating to their married life in LA.

Allie:

Looking back, we praise God for His divine guidance. If we decided to get married even a few months later—it might have been further delayed as Covid-19 took the world by surprise. There were times when my family would ask, "Are you sure you want to get married in January?" I would respond, "Yes, we believe that this is God's timing. What if something happens where we can't get married?" I had no idea that it would have been Covid-19, but God knew.

Wedding Preparation

Barnabas:

My two main tasks were to find a place to live and to buy a car. These tasks were very difficult for me back then. I didn't know much about cars as I mainly lived in countries that had great public transportation and little need for personal vehicles. Not having a car also made my search for a home difficult.

Still, the Lord blessed me greatly in my search for a lodging place and vehicle. I was able to find a studio through my college connections. Moreover, once the landlord knew I was a Bible and seminary student, she happily let me survey the place and was willing to offer me a deal. The studio was even furnished and minutes away from Biola University, allowing me to easily access classes and work.

However, the initial rent was still a problem for us. We prayed and asked if she could lower the rent by $100. She said she could lower it by $50, so we prayed even more. Six days later, she initiated a conversation and said that she was willing to lower the amount by $100—an answered prayer! Our first married home had been secured.

As for my search for a car, that proved to be more troubling than finding a place. I knew how to drive, but that's pretty much it.

55

I didn't know anything else and I received a lot of useful, yet conflicting information about which car to get. I was initially going to buy a Prius, but I was somehow drawn to a Scion XB.

There were a few that caught my attention. I contacted both owners but was left with no reply. Yet, on a Thursday morning, I was able to find one that was cheaper than the others with far less mileage. I hurriedly scheduled a test drive that afternoon and found the owner nice and gracious. He was even willing to lower the price knowing that I was a believer and wanted to serve in ministry. Four days later, I bought my first car, a 2013 Scion XB with less than 80,000 miles for $4800—and I didn't realize how good a deal it was!

Allie:

Life was no longer boring and mundane—but chaotic and stressful. I began working two jobs, from 6am till 10pm to save up for our wedding and our future. Every day felt short, and all my scarce free time was used for wedding planning. *I'm getting married in nearly 2 months! Jesus, I desperately need Your help!* And He did help me.

Initially, we were planning to get married minimalistically on a beach. We would mostly invite our immediate family. But Barnabas felt that we should get married in a church or chapel, representing our relationship with God and how we wanted to be joined together as a holy union in His presence. I started searching for a church for our wedding. After calling seven different churches, He opened the door for a beautiful, reasonably-priced venue. In fact, we even prayed for a specific price, and the venue was offered for that exact amount.

A lot of small yet providential things happened between September and our final encounter before getting married. I recorded it all down in a journal account:

> Dear Lord Jesus,
> I am amazed by You. I have been so doubtful, fearful, ungrateful and grumpy. Yet You continue to pour out Your

abundant blessings. Here are some of the things that You have done. You completely led Barnabas to propose to me. You gave us a church to get married in and a reception at a lower cost, including tables, chairs, and audio.

Debbie offered her house for our friends. My parents paid for church, food, wedding dress, and flowers, and Barnabas's parents' hotel. My friends from college will help out with worship. Shellese offered to help with wedding planning.

Barnabas's parents gave us $2000 to buy a car. A friend offered to give all of her items from her wedding to us. Barnabas's relatives and friends gave us $3000. Aunty Katherine gave $1200 for our wedding.

Wow, this is all Your doing. You work through the hearts of man. You are in control for You are God and Your grace is truly sufficient.

Barnabas & Allie:

Our four months of engagement went by quickly. It was occasionally a time filled with internal conflict as we wanted time to pass by quicker so that we could get married. Yet, we also wanted time to slow down, as we had all sorts of responsibilities and tasks to accomplish before meeting each other again.

Thankfully, the time difference between LA and Kona was two hours. This meant that we could talk and video-call without worries of interruption. Barnabas also had a phone plan that allowed for video calls. As time passed, we started to envision what our marriage would be like—only for us to realize it was far better and more exciting than anything we expected.

Chapter 8

What is Sex for?

WHILE SOME PEOPLE THINK that sex is great, others may say "sex is bad." Those who assert that "sex is for reproduction" may be objected with "no, sex is for pleasure." We can assure you there are probably endless descriptions about sex and its function.

All these descriptions about sex are valid, even if some of them contradict each other, because they are usually subjective descriptions of sex based on people's experiences. These descriptions do not define sex, nor do they illustrate the nature of sex. The objectivity of what sex is has not been changed by what people think about sex.

So, what is sex?

Here's a simple yet sufficient definition:

"Sex (the act and experience of sexual intercourse) is for marriage."

That's all that there is. Since this is a Christian book, the biblical basis will be provided, but if you have been raised Christian, please don't let this statement confuse you with some of the stuff about sex that you may have been hearing as you were raised. We're not providing you an opinion, that sex *should* be saved for marriage or giving you the imperative, "don't have sex before marriage!" Just as a fish can't survive out of water, sex can't find meaning outside of marriage. We're saying that the definition of sex is intrinsically tied to marriage—sex *is* for marriage. Sex *is not* for anything else—and only on this basis can we establish any true claims about sex.

Two Analogies

Suppose you were dating someone amazing, highly approved by your parents, and you had a dream car. One day, your dad comes up to you and asks you to follow him to the garage. Once you step in, you see your dream car parked there with the keys in his hand. This is what he tells you: "Son, this car is yours and here's the key. But please, don't drive it until you've married her."

You're left with two choices. You could wait till marriage, and then enjoy the ride together, or you could take the car for a quick spin. Or you could propose to her while driving across a beach during sunset. Or you could just use the car from this point onwards regardless of whatever happens between you and her. Should you wait for marriage and honor your dad in doing so? Probably. But could you start driving the car immediately? Why not? What other ramifications or consequences are there, aside from potentially breaking your dad's heart? There's nothing morally wrong in the act of driving the car that was meant as a gift; in fact, a car is meant to be driven.

This analogy is used to respond to those who only tell others to "save sex until marriage," or "don't have sex before marriage" without providing a basis. Sure, one can refrain from doing so until then, but why? An application, exhortation, or suggestion that does not have a basis is weak, ineffective, and powerless. In the same way, a claim that does not provide a basis for the ontological function of sex is ineffective and powerless unless the audience somehow blindly obeys everyone one says without a hint of suspicion.

Consider another analogy. Your parents buy you your dream car, but it only comes with a manual transmission and you only know how to drive automatic transmission. Somehow, instead of learning how to drive stick, you thought it was a good idea to start driving in 3rd or 4th gear instead of 1st. Not only will the car be barely able to move, starting at a high gear will likely damage the vehicle's transmission. In this scenario, there are real ramifications and consequences. Why? Because a car is designed and functioned to start a lower gear. This is the basis of how it's made and of how it works.

In the same way, whenever we talk about sex, we have to start with a definition—a basis—and then work our way up. The basis of sex is that it is for marriage.

LOGICAL ARGUMENTS

When someone says: "sex is for reproduction" or "sex is for pleasure," what they are not saying is that "sex is reproduction" or "sex is pleasure." Rather, they are saying that sex *results* in reproduction, the creating of a baby, and/or pleasure. In other words, reproduction or pleasure is an effect of sex.

On the other hand, sex is not for reproduction because almost anyone can reproduce with anyone of the opposite sex, assuming that the woman can still give birth. But clearly, no one with a sound mind would simply have sex with someone of the opposite sex just to reproduce, right?

Those who desire to reproduce through sex generally do so within the boundaries of marriage, or at least a committed relationship. We don't know anyone not in a committed relationship and *wants to* reproduce and raise a child as a potential parent or single parent. We haven't even touched on the side-effects, damage, and trauma caused by reproduction through sex by people who are not in committed relationships.

Is sex for pleasure? Sure, sex can certainly be pleasurable in the moment, maybe even for people who are not in marriage or committed relationships. But at the same time, is sex really pleasurable when it is performed outside of committed relationships such as marriage? Can anyone guarantee that? Can sex be pleasurable when it's performed in an unsafe environment? What about all the unknown components such as depression, guilt, shame, and remorse that may follow? Certainly, the idea of STDs isn't pleasurable, right?

Some people reading this might immediately fire back, saying: "Aren't there are many couples who have sex and still experience pleasure even though they are not married?"

Here's our response. But before that, please know that we're not writing this to condemn anyone. Believe it or not, we are writing this to be loving because we reasonably believe that sex outside of marriage isn't wise nor good for anyone's well-being. Honestly, we want you to experience sex for what it's worth, and that's within marriage. But as for this question, we don't deny that there are many unmarried couples who may experience pleasure during sex. But even though they aren't officially married, oftentimes their relationships are shaped in a way that is functionally married. Meaning, they try to live their lives as if they are married without using the language of marriage. They do everything similar to a married couple would do: they live together, they share finances and dreams, have children—but they aren't married. They might not be officially committed to each other as a married couple would, but they are not far away as well.

Maybe we all have an idea of what an absolutely committed relationship looks like, and the closer one is to that relationship—marriage—the more sex becomes pleasurable, enjoyable, and stress-releasing. This point can be asserted when you try imagining the stress and worry of being pregnant, when a woman has sex with another without commitment.

Moving on to Scripture, it seems clear that the Bible presents sex as for marriage as well. Let's briefly take a look at (1) the Creation account, (2) Mosaic Law, and (3) the New Testament.

Creation

The most essential truths about humanity and sexuality have to be grounded in the Creation account as this logic is displayed by Christ (cf. Mk 10:6–9) and the apostles (cf. 1 Cor 6).

Let's start with Adam and Eve. Adam and Eve are not only representative of humanity, but they are also archetypes of marriage, as Genesis 2 and 3 transitions from describing them as "man" and "woman", to "husband" and "wife" respectively (Gen 2:21-25). But how did they become husband and wife? Did God just miraculously create them as husband and wife? What about their marriage certificate?

The answer is found in Genesis 2:24, which writes: "Therefore a man shall leave his father and his mother and hold fast to his wife, and *they shall become one flesh*." "One flesh" or "one body" depicts sex. Sex is what joins a man to a woman, and they become one body. This is exceptionally clear in 1 Corinthians 6:16 (we'll get there eventually) when Paul quotes this verse in Gen 2:24 to depict sex. So how was Adam married to Eve? They had sex, which points to the notion that sex is for marriage.

Mosaic Law

During the time where the Mosaic Law (or "the Law") was in effect, which is the entire Old Testament since the middle of Exodus, sex is portrayed as for marriage. Leviticus 18 alone shows that the act and experience of sexual intercourse is only for one's wife or husband. However, please note that the Law does not apply to us today. When Jesus came in the New Testament, He fulfilled and abolished the Law. However, even though Leviticus 18 doesn't apply to us, we see that it continues what God has ordained for sex to be from the Creation account—that sex is for marriage.

Let's spice things up a bit. Go to Deuteronomy 22:28-30, in which this story will be paralleled with 2 Samuel 13:1-19. In short, the Deuteronomy 22 passage writes that if a man forces himself sexually on a woman, that he rapes her, he has violated the woman. Yet, this woman shall be his wife. Isn't that crazy? How can this make sense and what about her rights? There's much to discuss about this and praise God that the Law doesn't apply to us now, but the point is clear: God has decreed sex to be the marker that transitions one from being single to being married. Sex is what joins you to another person as both of you become one flesh.

As for 2 Samuel 13:1–19, here's what happened. One of David's sons was lusting for his half-sister, and he literally did what was written in Deuteronomy 22; he raped her (13:14). Some readers may not even know that this story is in the Bible. But after that, he was so evil that he told her to get out of his presence (13:15). But she said this: "No, my brother, for this wrong in sending me away is greater than the other that you did to me." (13:16)

If you go back five verses, before he raped her, Amnon actually invited his sister to have sex (13:11). She declined (13:12), saying that this is wrong, but told him to ask their father David if they could be married (13:13). So, we see that even among this great evil that was committed in Israel, there was still this strong association between sex and marriage, that sex is for marriage. Sex was not just seen as a random physical and emotional experience, but intentionally for marriage. If you go to verse 19, after Tamar was kicked out by her terrible brother, Scripture writes that she "put ashes on her head and tore the long robe that she wore."

Well, what does that mean? Putting ashes on her head was a symbolic act of grief and perhaps even widowhood. Even though they weren't officially married, the fact that Amnon cast her out after sexually assaulting her was as if she had been divorced or if she was a widow. Perhaps this touches upon what some people call a "soul tie"? Perhaps sex binds the soul of two people together and creates a bond that is only fitting for marriage.

Again, the passages in the Old Testament do not necessarily apply to us today as Jesus fulfilled the OT and everyone in Him is a New Creation. Still, The Old Testament adheres to the function of sex demonstrated from the Creation account, that sex is for marriage.

New Testament

Let's look at two brief passages in the New Testament.

In 1 Corinthians 7, it says that our bodies aren't even our own, but our spouses (7:3-4). Your body is reserved for your spouse or your future spouse if you're single. Your body is sexually reserved for marriage.

If you go back one chapter to 1 Corinthians 6, it is written:

> "Do you not know that your bodies are members of Christ? Shall I then take the members of Christ and make them members of a prostitute? Never! Or do you not know that he who is joined to a prostitute becomes one body with her? For, as it is written, "The two will become one flesh." (6:15-16)

In this passage, Paul goes all the way back to the Creation order and says that sex is the joining of two people as one body—one flesh—which is only suitable for marriage. Now Paul doesn't say that the person you have sex with, even if a prostitute, is the person you have to marry as the focus is verse 20, which writes: "glorify God with your body."

Still, sex is for marriage and sex is meant to be a core marker of the committed, loving relationship of marriage that is actually closest to God's image. Only under the basis that sex is for marriage, can we establish any logical and consistent claim regarding sex's function. In other words, if you take away sex from marriage, you cannot establish any logically consistent claim about sex.

Sex as Marriage Marker

Sex is for marriage. Since sex is made by God for the male and female in a marriage covenant, whenever a married couple engages in sexual activity, it is a renewal of their marriage vows and covenant. This is why sex within marriage is the most powerful, beautiful, and enjoyable. Because sex is a marriage marker, this serves as the basis to why sex in marriage is holistically powerful, beautiful, and enjoyable. Sex in marriage isn't just great physically, emotionally, or mentally in a stand-alone way, but it is spiritually renewing because it is ordained by God and ultimately glorifies God. Sex being performed under the boundaries of love in marriage allows the experience to result in pleasure, spiritual and emotional connection, increase in confidence, and even reproduction.

At the end of the day, unless God has called you to singleness, which is a blessing as Paul writes in 1 Corinthians 7, you are called to marriage. Those called to marriage are called to enjoy sex and to "eat its choicest fruits" (Song 4:16) in the garden of love—but only in marriage.

Chapter 9

Third Encounter

BARNABAS:

It was December 20th, 2019, five days before I flew out to meet my bride-to-be. I moved out of the dormitory into our new home. I spent the past two days busy packing and unpacking. I also had to complete all the grading for my professors. Through a mixture of fatigue and spiritual attack, I became very ill. At the height of my sickness, I couldn't talk and was coughing out blood.

ALLIE:

Barnabas is coming soon! I can't believe it! He's safely in our new home but he has some sort of cold. The text messages and calls ceased. I was getting irritated. *What's wrong? Is he that sick?* I actually didn't know how sick he was until a month later when I found blood stains. That was disgusting and we deep-cleaned everything.

BARNABAS:

I was all alone in a cold studio with no one to talk to. I couldn't talk to anyone anyway. Food became an issue. I didn't quite know

Third Encounter

how to cook, nor did I have any cookware. I was so weak I couldn't drive to get food. There were nights where I only ate a boiled egg and an apple. There were even a few nights where I couldn't sleep as my body was overheating and feverish. For a moment, I wondered if I could make it to my wedding.

In distress, I called my parents and asked them to pray for me. They prayed and proclaimed words of faith—that I would make it to the wedding—and those words pushed me on. I believed and recounted all the amazing things He had done in our relationship. He would protect me and fly me safely to Hawaii.

Allie:

It was December 25th, the long-awaited day. We were finally going to meet again after four long months. The weather was quite muggy and a bit gloomy. I desperately scrambled, trying to make warm food for him to eat as I expected that he must be hungry.

I picked him up from the airport and realized how sick he was. He couldn't talk much because his throat was sore, and he was very fatigued from the flight. This was the third time I met Barnabas Kwok, and this time, I was marrying him.

Barnabas:

Shortly after I arrived, my parents came over too. This fulfilled one of Uncle David's predictions during the first encounter, "This time you [Barnabas] meet us [Allie's parents], next time Allie meets your parents, and the next time, both parents meet."

Allie:

I was again feeling overwhelmed with the number of tasks to complete before getting married. We were able to do some activities together as soon-to-be one joint family. We drove to the other side of the island, Barnabas and I in one car, and my parents and future parents-in-law in another. This gave both our parents time to bond and get to know one another. I saw the start of a close friendship between our families. In fact, to this day, they still keep in touch with each other!

Fast-forward to the last day of 2019, 3 days before our wedding, I was once again panicking. We were busy putting together all the wedding favors.

I'm the type of person who likes to procrastinate only to have a sudden burst of energy to get things done at the last minute. With the amount of work we had to do, there was no way I could finish this on my own. I broke out of my comfort zone and asked for our parents' help in making our party favors. To this day, I have a sweet video I recorded on my phone of both our parents singing "Give Thanks" as they assembled all the bags.

Barnabas:

Allie's siblings arrived shortly and graciously helped us prepare for our wedding. We all had a meal together and they helped us out the most that one day before our wedding. That afternoon, Allie and I found ourselves exhausted and sleep deprived, yet we had to make dinner plans for both our families. As we were looking up catering we received a call from Debbie, one of Allie's church friends who was also helping us at our wedding. She asked if we had any dinner plans, and if we didn't, she offered to host both of our entire families at their place.

Surprised and overjoyed, we gratefully accepted their gracious offer. That night, I met Rick and Debbie as well as some of the Biola friends who came over for our wedding! Not only did they help out at our wedding, they even helped out with the cooking that night! Many of them were close friends with Allie, and this was the first time they met in almost two years. We had a wonderful meal at a much-needed time. Even at the last minute before our wedding, God knew our needs and weariness and showed us tremendous grace. Through this meal, God once again affirmed and told us that He is with us and that His grace is sufficient

Third Encounter

That night, the night before my big day, I slept at the hotel that my parents were staying in. I couldn't really sleep because I was still trying to process everything that had happened. Everything felt like a blur and I couldn't believe that my single, unmarried life was coming to an end—especially in a way that was not according to my plans. Everything was going to change tomorrow.

Yet, being with my parents that one night was a perfect way to conclude my singleness.

The Wedding Day—January 3rd, 2020

Barnabas:

It was around 7am. I woke up and took a shower, praying and praising God for everything that has happened in our lives and in this relationship. I couldn't believe I was hours away from being married. I carefully steamed my wedding tuxedo my parents had shipped over to me. They bought it for me without me trying it on as they knew my measurements.

Allie:

I woke up early in the morning only to find myself hearing my family running around the house, scrambling for the wedding. "Allie, where's the cake topper?" *What! I don't have time to think about this. I'm getting married in a few hours!*

We started driving to the hair salon. My sister looks down at mother's shoes: "Mom, there's no way you're wearing those to the wedding, right?" My mom looked down at her tan-colored sandals. "What's wrong with these?" she replied. "No mom, you can't wear those. They're ugly and they don't match with your dress. I'm going to buy you a pair of new shoes."

"Emi!" I growled, "it doesn't matter! We're going to the salon and I'm getting my hair and make-up done." Spoiler alert, my sister left during my appointment to buy new shoes for my mom. Another spoiler alert, I, the bridezilla, wasn't happy about that.

69

Barnabas:

Before heading out to the wedding venue, I prayed with my parents. They prayed their blessing over me, and I prayed a powerful prayer. Being filled with God's peace and presence, I prayed that God would glorify His name today in that chapel. I prayed that this wedding won't just be about us, but Him. I prayed that this wedding, perhaps a rare occasion for some people to come to a church building, would change their hearts and minds towards Jesus Christ. *Lord, may you use this wedding for Your glory!*

Allie:

As I was getting my make-up done, the beautician asked me: "Oh, so when's the ceremony?" only for me to respond: "In an hour." Her eyes widened. "What! It takes two hours for hair and makeup. Oh no!" I internally facepalmed thinking about the email I sent her months ago that contained the date and time of the ceremony. I felt her nervousness so I said: "Oh, it will be okay," only to find my eyebrows as thick as a caterpillar. *Oh no, I can't be walking down the aisle like this.*

My sister came back, and she began giggling at my makeup and took pictures. *Thanks, Emi. Thanks so much.* My mom took a phone call on speaker. I heard the panicked voices and snarled: "Mom, take the phone call outside. I can't listen to this."

Barnabas:

My parents and I arrived at the chapel around 9am, an hour before the ceremony began. It was surreal. I was first amazed by everyone who volunteered to help us and those who delegated the entire process—they just knew what to do automatically and set the place up perfectly. My family and I were surprised by how smooth everything went even though most of them didn't know each other before that morning.

Second, I was filled with emotion when I saw many wonderful and faithful friends. I saw my best friends who flew all the way from Hong Kong and the friends I met at college who flew over from Los Angeles.

After talking and greeting those present, I spent the remaining time standing near the altar area with pastor Danny, our officiating pastor. He spoke many encouraging words of kindness, many of which I still remember as they gave me calmness and composure.

Allie:

It was around 9:45am. My hair and makeup were eventually complete. We drove home so I could put on my wedding dress. I saw my dad wearing his plain clothes, "Dad! What are you wearing? I'm getting married in 10 minutes." The wedding venue was less than 5 minutes away from where we lived. Still, even though I'm known for being laid back, this just wasn't the day!

Finally, we arrived at the church. As soon as I stepped out, I was greeted by a family friend who helped coordinate everything. She began speaking kind words and they gave me lots of peace. Suddenly, everything felt unreal. The months of worrying, the sleepless nights, and the hair-pulling moments all melted away. Today was the day where I was going to marry Barnabas Kwok.

Barnabas:

It was past 10am and Allie had yet to arrive. Pastor Danny reassured me, "Don't worry, no weddings in Hawaii are on-time." I genuinely appreciated his comforting words, but I wasn't worried. I was simply trying my best to take everything in and enjoy this momentous, once-in-a-lifetime occasion.

Around 15 minutes later, I was told that Allie had arrived. The ceremony began, and I walked my parents to their place at the front of the chapel. Allie's parents also walked in as well, sitting directly across my parents. Uncle David, or, as I called him then, "Mr. Yamakawa," walked back outside to bring Allie inside this beautiful chapel.

Our Best Life before the Best Life

The music began.

Allie:

For the first time, my dad and I walked arm-in-arm. Let me say this about my family: we're not the most expressive in our affection. But in this moment, I felt how great my father's love was for me. As I began to enter the chapel, behind my veil, I saw the faces of everyone who has been there for me throughout my entire life. I kept crying as we walked down the aisle to the song "As the Deer." Once we arrived at the front, facing Barnabas and pastor Danny, my dad unveiled me, kissed me on my cheek, and responded, "Her mother and I do" to the pastor's question "Do you let this woman be married to this man?"

Barnabas:

There she was—my bride stood right in front of me. Everything was still a blur. *Is this really happening? I can't believe we're getting married.* I could only stare at her while trying to keep myself from crying.

The worship started. Our friends Ryan and Kelly led the worship that I coordinated months earlier. As the chapel echoed with praise and I saw Allie's hands lifted up in worship, I couldn't contain it anymore. I tried to sing but I was filled with a strong presence and peace of the Holy Spirit that my vocal cords couldn't function properly. Uncontrollable tears started rolling down my cheeks as I could do nothing but praise God for this very moment.

Allie:

As we were worshiping the Lord, I only had praise on my lips for Him. Before I even heard of Barnabas, I would ask my mom every night to pray for my future husband. I would lay on her lap and she would stroke my hair and pray, "Oh Lord Jesus, I pray that Allie would marry a godly man, amen." It was a very simple, yet powerful prayer. Soon, her prayers began to change from "a godly man" to "I hope she can meet that nice, young man, Barnabas."

Today, I saw my mom's prayers being fulfilled.

Barnabas:

We then proceeded to take communion in the presence of all the witnesses. In the midst of the solemnity, we encountered a funny moment. We proceeded to the communion table that was placed at the side of the altar. This was the nicest communion silverware we've seen and naturally, we would take the cup before the bread.

However, the cups were labelled "you" and "me." We were giggling and stood there for a minute whispering: "Who's you and who's me?" Well, we couldn't keep everyone waiting forever, so I was "me" and Allie was "you."

Allie:

Shortly after communion, Barnabas read his vows to me.

> "Ephesians 5:25–28 writes:
>
> "Husbands, love your wives, as Christ loved the church and gave himself up for her, that he might sanctify her, having cleansed her by the washing of water with the word, so that he might present the church to himself in splendor, without spot or wrinkle or any such thing, that she might be holy and without blemish. In the same way, husbands should love their wives as their own bodies. He who loves his wife loves himself."
>
> Jesus died for you and me, for His church, for His bride. But His death marked the beginning—not the end of His love. Jesus died for His bride so that she may be sanctified, cleansed, and presented in splendor, holy and without blemish.
>
> I am a child of God, that's the most important identity of my life. And as a Christian I have died, and it is Christ who lives in me.
>
> But today, Allie, in the presence of God and His people, I give my life to you.

I take you to be my wife, to share with you God's plan for us. I vow to lead you as the head of the family as we both submit to Jesus' headship. I will not speak any bad to you.

I proclaim that I will love you—I will seek your well-being—by giving you everything in health and in sickness, in joy and sorrow, until death do we part.

All these I pledge to in the Name of the Father, Son, and Holy Spirit.

Allie, I love you.

Barnabas:

As I slipped my vows back into my pocket, Allie began her vows. This was the most touching moment of the entire ceremony.

"The first week we started dating you asked me, 'Do you believe that God loves you?' I was pierced by this question. As a Christian, even though I had the knowledge that Jesus loves me, sometimes it was hard to believe.

For a while I viewed God as the wrathful Judge, who is ready to strike me down with bolts of lightning the minute I make a mistake. Condemnation and doubt from my former years haunted me. I was scared to open up to you and share my ugly past. I thought that if I told you, you would surely run away in disgust.

So one night, I mustered up the courage to tell you everything. I felt so vulnerable and ashamed of previous sins I have committed. I thought to myself, will Barnabas still love me? Will he still be able to see me the same?

And then after pouring out my heart to you, you replied, 'Allie. You're one of the most pure girls I know. Jesus has made you into a new creation and that's all I see. Allie, He has made you into a new creation!'

Through this relationship, Jesus used you, Barnabas, to show me an everlasting and pure love that is given and not earned. Through you the Lord has shown me that I am a new creation, I have been washed clean by the blood of Jesus. Through you God has affirmed His love for me over and over again showing me that I am a precious daughter of the Most High King.

I can't thank God enough for you. You have been the biggest influence and Christ-like figure in my life. Thank you for fully loving and accepting me. Thank you for making me feel beautiful. Thank you for relentlessly showing me grace, kindness, and gentleness. I am so in love with you and I give all the glory and praise to my first and true love, Almighty Jesus. Amen and Amen."

Barnabas, I vow to love you all the days of my life. I vow to bless you and not curse you. I will not gossip about you to others, but rather bring my burdens to God in prayer. As Jesus has shown me mercy, kindness, and forgiveness, so will I do for you. I vow to be a faithful, pure, and devoted wife, keeping my eyes, thoughts, and heart on you alone. As your helper, I will share your burdens. As your cheerleader I will encourage and support you. As your best friend I will laugh and cry with you. As your wife I will submit and respect you. As your sister in Christ I will fervently pray for you and speak words of faith. I will follow you to the ends of the earth wherever God calls you.

I love you, Barnabas.

Allie:

Shortly after that, we were pronounced husband and wife. Here's the big moment that our friends and family have been waiting for: the kiss. As we have mentioned earlier, we decided to never kiss, not on the cheeks or the lips, until the day of our wedding. All eyes were fixed on us only to see Barnabas kiss me on the cheeks. What followed was a cheerful but unsatisfied reaction.

Someone yelled: "Come on, kiss her!" I instantly responded, "That's for later," spurring an even greater reaction from everyone there.

Barnabas & Allie:

We walked out the beautiful chapel as a married couple. We then stood outside, greeting everyone who came to our one and only special day. That moment signified countless answered prayers as God testified His power and sovereignty in joining us through the most miraculous signs and wonders.

We sat at our designated table, trying to fully enjoy every passing second. We were filled with joy and awe, struck with disbelief regarding our new identities as a married couple. We were also filled with gratitude as we saw countless people's efforts in making our wedding day as amazing as possible.

One thing that was rather unfortunate was that we didn't try the food that we ordered—we simply did not have the appetite at that moment. Yet, until this day, we always wondered what the food tasted like as it was really well received. Oh well.

Not long after, we left for the beach with Frank—Barnabas's close friend who came all the way from Hong Kong—as he snapped some wonderful photos of us in our wedding attires. We then headed back to our hotel and began our honeymoon. And yes, the actual kissing started there.

Chapter 10

The Best Life

MARRIAGE IS AN INDICATOR of the best life that one will have. Don't worry, this doesn't mean that single people out there are hopeless. The call to singleness (cf. Matt 19:20; 1 Cor 7) becomes more prominent under the New Covenant as Jesus reveals that there is no marriage in heaven (Matt 22:20). In fact, Jesus Himself demonstrates this as He lived as a single man on earth. Yet, He also lived the best and most fulfilling life through a perfectly loving and holy relationship with God. His example should speak volumes.

But what is marriage for if there is no marriage in heaven? Why did God establish marriage only as a temporal phenomenon?

God, in His infinite knowledge and wisdom, could give us a one-liner definition and explanation. But if He did so, would we understand what He is talking about? Probably not. Maybe this is why there's a term known as "progressive revelation." This means that God progressively reveals Himself and the things pertaining to His Kingdom over time. For example, animal sacrifices in the Law (e.g.: Lev 1; 3–7) were also a temporary phenomenon for the Israelites. They were commanded by God to offer animal sacrifices as an atonement for their sins (and other things). Yet, an animal's blood could not truly take away one's sins (Heb 10:1–4). Rather, they served as pointer to Christ's atoning, propitiatory sacrifice (cf. Rom 3:25; Heb 7:27; 1 John 2:2; 4:10). Thus, Christ's sacrifice "does away with the first [offerings and sacrifices—those of animals]." (Heb 10:9)

In the same way, God established marriage—the loving, relational union between a husband and wife—as a foretaste and pointer to the ultimate relationship that we will experience with God in heaven. This is a relationship that does not have the mars of sin, sorrow, and shame.

Marriage in Genesis 1–3

Let's start from the Creation account. God created humanity, represented by male and female, in His Image (Gen 1:26–27). Just from this simple statement, we can see that God's Image is reflected by both genders. A man reflects the Image of God and so does a woman—though they are different! Moving on to Genesis 2, Scripture describes the man and woman as "husband and wife" (or "the man and his wife") (2:22–25).

God created man and woman for marriage, in which one purpose is so that they can "be fruitful and multiply and fill the earth and subdue it..." (1:28): reproduction. Just as the first revelatory identity that God reveals is that He is creator, God's Image—man and woman in a marital relationship—also creates through reproduction. The ability to reproduce another being also in the Image of God, through sex in a marital relationship, reflects God.

Furthermore, marriage is instituted as a union *in relationship with God*. Even though the Old Testament does not reveal God as the Trinity, in which the Father is having a perfect relationship with the Son and Spirit, Adam and Eve were living in the garden of Eden in the presence of God in relationship with Him without any hindrances of sin and shame. God, Adam, and Eve were in a near-perfect relationship—until humanity was kicked out of Eden—where the couple could even hear the sound of God walking (3:8) and had unhindered communication with Him (3:3; 3:9–19). Perhaps this reflects the relationship God has with Himself. Obviously, the incoming of sin through humanity's fall renders such a relationship impossible until the new heaven and earth (cf. Rev

21). If anything, the fact that marriage was instituted in relationship with God implies the spiritual connection a couple should have with God and reflects the perfect relationship that God has with Himself.

Marriage in Ephesians 5

This is one of the most famous passages that illustrates the complementarian roles shared between a husband and wife's relationship in marriage. Some of you might be aware that there are diverging opinions surrounding complementarianism and egalitarianism in marriage. We won't dive deep into that debate here. However, we simply believe that God created man and woman as equals, but with some different roles and functions. Hence, we believe and apply what this passage writes concerning what a husband and wife should do in marriage.

Following the flow and logic in the passage, let's start with the wives:

> "Wives, submit to your own husbands, as to the Lord. For the husband is the head of the wife even as Christ is the head of the church, his body, and is himself its Savior. Now as the church submits to Christ, so also wives should submit in everything to their husbands." (Eph 5:22–24)

Perhaps contrary to some popular or cultural notions, Paul exhorts the wives to submit to their husbands. Please note that Paul tells the wives to submit to their husbands, not just to any men. This is an in-house, family issue. Paul exhorts wives to do so *not* because husbands carry more intrinsic worth nor are they more gifted. Rather, the call to submission is "as to the Lord," (5:22) indicating authority. In other words, Paul tells the wives to submit to their husbands as they have greater authority in a family—just as the believers of God submits to Christ (5:24) as He is the Head of the church (Col 1:18) with all authority.

Paul then addresses the husbands:

"Husbands, love your wives, as Christ loved the church and gave himself up for her, that he might sanctify her, having cleansed her by the washing of water with the word, so that he might present the church to himself in splendor, without spot or wrinkle or any such thing, that she might be holy and without blemish. In the same way husbands should love their wives as their own bodies. He who loves his wife loves himself. For no one ever hated his own flesh, but nourishes and cherishes it, just as Christ does the church, because we are members of his body. 'Therefore a man shall leave his father and mother and hold fast to his wife, and the two shall become one flesh.' This mystery is profound, and I am saying that it refers to Christ and the church. However, let each one of you love his wife as himself, and let the wife see that she respects her husband." (5:25–33)

Husbands, on the other hand, are called to love their wives—not just in a general way as a married couple would naturally love each other—but in a specific way. They are called to love their wives "as Christ loved the church" (5:25) and died for her. As Jesus says that the greatest love is to lay down one's life for another (John 15:13), husbands are commanded to do so for their wives. This passage does not just instruct the husbands to die for their wives if necessary, but to love them with the greatest love possible. They are called to love their wives in the most self-sacrificial and selfless manner. Guess what? This specific love has first been demonstrated by God for the church, and the husband is to follow suit.

Thus, if there's anything that we can glean about this passage with regards to marriage, we see that the relationship of a husband and wife is also supposed to reflect God! The wife is supposed to reflect God through submission, as the church submits to Christ and Christ submits to the Father (cf. Matt 26:39; John 6:36; 10:18; 14:31; 15:10; Phil 2:8; Heb 5:8). The husband is supposed to reflect God through love, demonstrated by Christ for His bride. Marriage is a unique relationship on earth that best reflects some attributes and characteristics of God. Marriage reflects and points to God as it presents a taste of heaven!

Objection #1:

"I don't necessarily have an issue with submitting to my husband, and definitely no issues with submitting to Christ. But I don't understand why Scripture tells me to do so with the comparison between Jesus and my husband. There's no problem submitting to Christ as He's morally and lovingly perfect—but my husband isn't Jesus!"

It is true that a husband would never come close to who Jesus is. Jesus is perfect and a husband isn't. Yet a husband can at least be like God in his commitment of love for his wife—in the sense that Christ's love signified a new sanctified beginning for the church, "that she might be holy and without blemish" (Eph 5:27).

Objection #2:

What if a husband says: "this makes sense, but what if my wife does not submit nor respect me?" Or what if a wife says: "this makes sense, but what if my husband does not love me in a Christ-like way at all?" If this is the case, then the problem lies not with Scripture or God's ideal for marriage, but with people and their fallenness. There are some men and women who should not be, at least based on where they're currently at, one's respective husband or wife.

For example, let's say there was a family where the husband tried killing the wife and their children, resulting in the wife fleeing and permanently leaving the husband with the children. In that situation, the problem does not merely lie with submission or love, but life and death. Even though God's ideal for a married couple is "let no man separate" (Mk 10:12), it might not be morally good or loving for the wife and her children to stay with such a man, endangering herself and her little ones. Yet, notice how the reaction to such a situation is not directed at God and His decreed ideal—but to man and human fallenness. This is why our book includes a dating worksheet and a chapter on what love is, so that one can avoid fundamental relational and marital issues that oftentimes relate with unrefined character and maturity. After all, marriage is for mature men and women and not for immature boys and girls.

Objection #3:

Let's consider one last basic objection to the complementarian roles in marriage. What if one says, "I don't want to submit to my husband, why do I have to submit to him?" or "I don't want to love my wife, why do I have to love her?"

The truth is, a husband or wife does not *have* to do any of what Scripture mandates. Love, nor a good relationship, cannot be forced. Even in one's relationship with God, one cannot forcefully worship, love, and submit to Him as the Lord of one's life.

In fact, the flesh, our earthly tendencies, will naturally object to what God has decreed to be good because we aren't! It is wrong to assume that "I should submit to my husband" or "I should love my wife unconditionally" because it is "my natural desire to do so" or because "it's easy." On the other hand, have you considered that God decreed such a mandate because it is precisely difficult and counter-cultural? And because it is so, God has not given such mandates to those living in the flesh—but those in the Spirit! Through the Spirit who lives in His believers, the call to Christ-like submission and love is a precise way for the couple to allow God to dwell and move within their relationship. This makes marriage communal, not only between the husband and wife, but also with the Lord as He should be the foundation of every relationship. If humanity can naturally, as in, through the flesh, regulate a mutually loving and selfless relationship, a flourishing relationship would not require God's involvement.

MARRIAGE FOR GOD

Nonetheless, given that marriage is indeed temporal, as God establishes it as a foretaste and reflection of what heaven will be like when we're with God—the best life—this should impact one's motive in romantic relationships. First, given that marriage is a representation of God and His image, the pursuit of marriage should be aligned with one's pursuit of God. The two should be on the same track. One cannot pursue a holy union filled with unconditional love without pursuing God as He is the basis of love (refer to chapter 4). This is why we believe and can testify that true Christian marriages are better and more fruitful because a couple does not merely pursue their relationship by themselves, but through their union with God.

Second, given that marriage is a pointer to the upcoming best life, marriage is not an end in itself. In the Christian worldview through the basis of Scripture, marriage does not *result in* ultimate satisfaction—marriage *points to* ultimate satisfaction: the heavenly relationship we will have with God. Thus, anyone who marries, or pursues marriage with the hopes of finding ultimate satisfaction, will be greatly disappointed. Marriages on such bases will even fail, perhaps providing one reason for the rates of divorce and infidelity.

On the other hand, one who pursues marriage in one's pursuit of God and His righteousness will find a satisfaction that comes through the beauty of a holy union. Why? Because this satisfaction is not solely grounded within the relationship between the husband and wife—but through one's individual and communal relationship with God. As it is famously written in Matthew 6:31–33:

> "Therefore do not be anxious, saying, 'What shall we eat?' or 'What shall we drink?' or 'What shall we wear?' For the Gentiles seek after all these things, and your heavenly Father knows that you need them all. But seek first the kingdom of God and his righteousness, and all these things will be added to you."

We believe that God will provide your relational and marital needs and desires—even a spouse if you're single—if your utmost focus is on His Kingdom and righteousness.

The best life one experiences is not earthly marriage—but an upcoming heavenly marriage where we will all be joined to Christ as His bride. However, a married couple anchored in Christ will certainly taste glimpses of that best life on earth.

Chapter 11

Our Best Life

BARNABAS & ALLIE:

On January 9th, 2020, six days after our wedding, we boarded a flight back to Los Angeles to begin our newly-wed life. Three days later, we were hit by reality as Barnabas was back to being a full-time student and part-time student worker. Still, everything went relatively well during the first two months as we began to adapt to each other and live as a married couple.

Then COVID hit.

First, we were trapped in a 200 square feet (our estimation) studio. We repeat: a studio—one room only (and bathroom). Don't get us wrong, living in a studio wasn't bad, and it definitely served a time and season. We could literally see each other anywhere in the studio and this meant that, for the most part, we had complete transparency and had to do everything together. There was no separation. This became a lot more complicated when Barnabas had to work and study at home. Whenever Barnabas would be in class or tutoring his students, Allie would be in the background cooking or doing dishes.

Second, we started feeling immense financial pressure once it hit March as Allie had yet to find a job, and Barnabas could only make a limited amount of money as a student-worker. Allie tried her best and applied to various jobs, only to be rejected a "small" amount of 70 times. We repeat: 70 times! This hit our morale hard, especially Allie's. The amount of tears shed during that season was insurmountable. We rationed out all our food and ate sparingly, hoping to conserve every bit of food to the best that we could. The fact that many were losing their jobs didn't help, nor did some people's "advice" raise our spirits at all. We even lost weight. We were concerned, as Allie almost dropped to the same weight as she was in middle school.

Third, COVID didn't just hit us, but the entire world including our families. Not only were we locked in a studio with limited supplies, facing financial difficulties and unedifying advice, we were also concerned for our families. Barnabas's parents were then in Hong Kong facing general difficulties due to the pandemic, but also from a political change that was taking place. Allie's parents were also facing difficulties in adapting to the changes caused by COVID as well as some health issues. The fact that we were also helpless in doing anything substantial for our families made it more emotionally challenging.

In the midst of all those trials and tribulations, we still consider it our best life. Why? Obviously, not because we were living the American dream or in a fairytale. We had struggles with our environment, finances, and social life. Yet, just as John 16:33 writes:

> "I have said these things to you, that in me you may have peace. In the world you will have tribulation. But take heart; I have overcome the world."

Not only do we have each other—we have Jesus who supplies us a joy and peace that surpasses understanding. We have a King who is with us and loves us and works all things for good in accordance to His will for us as we love Him (cf. Rom 8:28). This is our best life because Jesus is with us.

Miraculous Interventions

Barnabas:

Let's start with something small, like a ring. Allie and I bought our respective wedding rings for ourselves, in which both of them had "Psalm 118" inscribed on them, recapturing one of God's signs for our relationship. Three weeks after we got married, we spontaneously decided to get a late bite around 2am. However, I realized my ring went missing once we arrived at the restaurant. I was freaking out and didn't enjoy our meal at all. In terms of monetary value, the ring didn't cost that much—but it was invaluable to me as it was my wedding ring and contained vast significance and memories.

I put on one of my spare rings the next day as I gloomily went to work. In that season, God blessed us greatly as we had post-marital counseling with a widely-respected and godly couple. After Allie and I met-up with that couple on the same day, I received a surprising package notification.

I retrieved and opened the package. Guess what? It was the same exact ring with the inscription "Psalm 118"! Allie and I were shocked. We definitely did not buy another ring, and even if we did, it would not arrive the next day. My ring took months to be made. I also did not receive any prior notification of an arriving ring. To this day, we have no idea of how that ring arrived—aside from how it was a miracle. God knew I was going to lose my ring and somehow, in His love and compassion, He ordered another one without my knowledge and payment.

Months later, I found my original ring in one of my bags. I didn't know how it got there, but I now have two identical rings with "Psalm 118". This experience boosted our faith and confidence in the Lord. Jesus is with us even in these "tiny" issues. Whenever I fidget my ring or gaze at it, I am reminded of His love, grace, and nearness. This ring also served as a reminder of His faithfulness as we were about to be hit with all the challenges and difficulties that came with COVID. This ring once again reminded me that God had ordained and affirmed our relationship and marriage. Jesus is with us in our marriage.

Allie:

It was painful to experience the rejection of over 70 workplaces. I didn't even want to apply anymore—I was so afraid of putting in my best efforts and getting rejected all over again. We also received discouraging comments from people, some telling me that I am foolish for moving out to Los Angeles with no set plan and others telling me that I am unqualified for the jobs I am applying to. I almost began to believe what people were telling me and truly wondered if we could continue living in Los Angeles.

One night as I was doing the dishes, I felt God telling me that I would get a job by the end of April. At that point, we had faced so much disappointment that Barnabas didn't even want to believe in this word. Still, I felt a sense of peace through it. Later that evening, Barnabas told me to apply as an Executive Assistant at a Christian bank. I was filled with rage. *How dare he tell me to apply for such a high position when I have been rejected everywhere.* Still, I angrily listened and applied. For the first time, instead of writing a dry and standard cover letter as I had been doing, I added in my own personality as I doubted they would even give me a second look.

We didn't receive any feedback so we decided to visit the bank and personally hand in my resume. In our brief time there, we were both amazed at how beautiful the campus was and noticed the various facilities that they offered. Among all the places that I applied to, this one had the best work environment. I thought to myself, *Would a fancy place like this even hire me?*

Two weeks later, I received a call from the Christian bank. They told me that they had a new job opening and would like to interview me! They hired me after two interviews and my starting date was April 28, 2020. At that moment, I remembered what God spoke to me about receiving a job by the end of April and burst into tears.

Even when I was so faithless, God was so faithful to me. My heart was filled with joy and gratitude for His providence.

Communication and Emotional Health

Barnabas & Allie:

Jesus wasn't only with us through crazy and miraculous events, as mentioned above, He is with us on a daily basis that surrounds the mundaneness of every life as husband and wife.

Barnabas:

A type of question we receive all the time is: "Do you fight?" or "How often do you fight?" We never quite know how to answer these questions because everyone defines "fighting" differently. What does it mean to "fight"? Is "fighting" having different opinions, tension, conflicts, yelling, throwing furniture around, or a full-on cold war?

Naturally, two people being put together will eventually result in different and conflicting opinions and preferences. That's not necessarily a problem. With conflicts come greater understanding and reconciliation. In fact, by God's grace, we have never gone to sleep in a conflict or moody mood. We always resolve our conflicts and head to sleep in a "cuddly" mood. If we have disagreements, we talk it out lovingly and graciously—always looking to understand the other side before issuing a response.

Furthermore, more reconciliation and resolved conflicts means that we get along better and better!

Allie:

For example, there was a time where a friend called me and only made hurtful and negative comments. Since I had the call on my phone's speaker and Barnabas and I were living in a studio, he heard everything. Barnabas was enraged throughout the call. Once the call ended, he was mad at me for not talking back to this person or trying to defend myself.

I was upset that he was mad at me. I have known my friend for a long time and from my perspective, I was trying to be a witness of Christ by not exchanging words back. But to Barnabas, he believed that there was a time to speak and be silent, and this was certainly a time to speak. He also came from the perspective of wanting to protect me.

Initially, we were both mad at each other as we shared two different perspectives. But after talking it out and by God's grace, we came to a mutual understanding and found a resolution. From that point onwards, Barnabas would answer the call with me whenever this person called. Perhaps being fearful of Barnabas, this person would not speak demeaning and hurtful things anymore knowing that Barnabas would speak out. This way, I could still connect with this friend while allowing Barnabas to jump in.

Barnabas & Allie:

We can honestly keep on going with examples of how Jesus has faithfully been with us all along in small and big issues as we held on to Him as our strength and refuge—trying our best in seeking His Kingdom and righteousness. Our best life is nowhere near the American dream nor do we have a lot to brag about when it comes to what we have, both monetarily and materialistically.

But we have Jesus. We are blessed, empowered, loved, prosperous, and protected because the King of kings and Lord of lords is with us and has saved us from the world and its lingering sins and worries. He has given us a new life and a new life together—a life filled with His love and presence; a life where sorrow can be turned into joy; a life that has no end as death is conquered and "is no more" (Rev 21:4). This is our best life because He lives and because He has been in the midst of our relationship from the beginning—and He will be with us as a married couple till the end.

An Ending?

That's the ending to this book. We'll admit, it's pretty abrupt because we've only been married for around two years. If anything, we are far closer to the beginning of our marital life and relationship than anything else. There's still so much for us to explore and go through as a married couple. Maybe we'll write a sequel in 20 years (if the opportunity arises) but we know that Jesus will continue to lead us in accordance with His calling and that no matter what, the best is yet to come.

At the same time, we would like to remind you that we are just ordinary people serving an extraordinary God. It's all about Him and this story reflects His work. This story points to His story. With that said, you can have a crazy story like ours too (if it isn't already crazy)—crazy in the sense that it is filled with God's providence and power; crazy in the sense that it is heavenly and heaven-like—because it is filled with God's presence.

If you're single and looking forward to marriage, I pray that this book was able to shed light on your quest for a spouse. Hopefully, there were some principles and tips that you could take away and apply to your life. If you're happily married in Christ, hopefully our story was able to encourage yours and that you could find joy in witnessing how the Lord works in other couples' lives—even ours!

Last but not least, if you're new to the Christian faith or if you have questions and doubts about God and the Bible, please reach out! You can reach out to us, a local church pastor, a trustworthy Christian friend (if you know one) or, even better, directly to God Himself! God is with you closer than you realize. As long as you open your heart and seek Him with all your heart, you will find Him and realize that a life with Christ is your best life.

www.ingramcontent.com/pod-product-compliance
Lightning Source LLC
Chambersburg PA
CBHW070306100426
42743CB00011B/2371